CONTENTS

KU-260-059

The phrase sections in this book are concise and to the point.
In each section you will find: a list of basic vocabulary; a
selection of useful phrases; a list of common words and
expressions that you will see on signs and notices. A full
pronunciation guide is given for things you'll want to say or
ask and typical replies to some of your questions are listed.

Of course, there are bound to be occasions when you want to
know more. So this book allows for this by giving an
English-Thai dictionary with a total of some 1,600 references.
This will enable you to build up your Thai vocabulary and to
make variations on the phrases in the phrase sections.

As well as this we have given a menu reader covering over 100
dishes and types of food - so that you will know what you
are ordering!

The section on Thailand and Things Thai gives cultural
information about Thailand as well as some notes on
the language.

Speaking the language can make all the difference to
your trip. So:

โชคดี
chôhk dee!
good luck!

เที่ยวสนุกนะ
têe-o sa-nÒOk ná!
have a good trip!

PRONUNCIATION

Thai words in this phrase book are given in both Thai script and a romanised form of pronunciation. If you read out the pronunciation as English words and pay attention to the tones, a Thai should be able to understand you. Some notes on the pronunciation system:

consonants

dt	a sharp 't' sound (somewhere between English 'd' and 't')
bp	a sharp 'b' sound (somewhere between English 'b' and 'p')
g	always hard as in 'get'
ng	as in 'bring', but can occur at the beginning of a word in Thai

vowels and vowel combinations

a	as in 'another'
e	as in 'den'
i	as in 'sin'
o	as in 'gone'
u	as in 'sun'
ah	as in 'rather'
ai	as in 'Thai'
air	as in 'fair'
ao	as in 'Mao'
ay	as in 'way'
ee	as in 'meet'
er	as in 'butter'
eu	rather like the 'ugh!' sound children make when forced to eat food they don't like!
ew	as in 'few'
oh	as in 'no'
oo	as in 'root'
OO	as in 'look'
oy	as in 'joy'

PRONUNCIATION

TONES

Each syllable in Thai is pronounced with a certain tone; two completely different words, such as mâi 'not' pronounced with a falling tone, and mái 'wood' often sound identical to the unaccustomed Western ear. It is therefore extremely important to pronounce words with the correct tone. There are five tones in Thai: the mid tone (no mark), the high tone (´), low tone (`), rising tone (ˇ) and falling tone (^). The mid-tone can be thought of as being similar to your normal voice pitch, with the low tone and high tone, being slightly lower and higher respectively; the rising tone is similar to the intonation used when asking a question like 'oh?' and the falling tone is like the rather emphatic intonation used when saying 'No!'

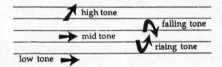

In the phrase sections and dictionary of this book, the words 'kâ', 'ká', 'dee-chún' or 'chún' in brackets replace the preceding word when the phrase is spoken by a female speaker.

hello
sa-wùt dee krúp (kâ)   สวัสดีครับ (ค่ะ)

hi
bpai nǎi krúp (kâ)   ไปไหนครับ (ค่ะ)

good morning/good evening
sa-wùt dee krúp (kâ)   สวัสดีครับ (ค่ะ)

pleased to meet you
yin dee têe dâi róo-jùk   ยินดีที่ได้รู้จัก

goodbye
lah gòrn ná   ลาก่อนนะ

cheerio
bpai ná   ไปนะ

see you
jer gun mài ná   เจอกันใหม่นะ

yes (see grammar)
krúp (kâ)   ครับ (ค่ะ)

no (see grammar)
mâi krúp (kâ)   ไม่ครับ (ค่ะ)

yes please
ao krúp (kâ)   เอาครับ (ค่ะ)

no thank you
mâi ao kòrp-kOOn   ไม่เอาขอบคุณ

please (asking for something)
kǒr ...   ขอ ...

please (asking someone to do
    something)
chôo-ay ...   ช่วย ...

9

GENERAL PHRASES

thank you/thanks
kòrp-kOOn

ขอบคุณ

thanks very much
kòrp-kOOn mâhk

ขอบคุณมาก

you're welcome
mâi bpen rai

ไม่เป็นไร

sorry *(apology)*
kŏr-tôht

ขอโทษ

sorry? *(didn't understand)*
a-rai ná?

อะไรนะ

how are you?
bpen yung-ngai bâhng?

เป็นอย่างไรบ้าง

very well, thank you
sa-bai dee, kòrp-kOOn

สบายดีขอบคุณ

and yourself?
láir-o kOOn lâ?

แล้วคุณล่ะ

excuse me *(to get attention)*
kŏr-tôht krúp (kâ)

ขอโทษครับ (ค่ะ)

how much is it?
tâo-rài?

เท่าไร

can I ...?
... dâi mái?

... ได้ไหม

can I have ...?
kŏr ...

ขอ ...

I'd like to ...
yàhk ja ...

อยากจะ ...

where is ...?
... yòo têe-năi?

... อยู่ที่ไหน

it's not (+ adjective) ...
mâi ...

ไม่ ...

10

GENERAL PHRASES

it's not (+ *noun*) ...
mâi châi ...

is it ...?
... châi mái?   ... ใช่ไหม

is there ... here?
têe-nêe mee ... mái?   ที่นี่มี ... ไหม

could you say that again?
chôo-ay pôot èek tee dâi mái?   ช่วยพูดอีกทีได้ไหม

could you speak more slowly?
chôo-ay pôot cháh cháh nòy dâi
        mái?   ช่วยพูดช้าๆหน่อยได้ไหม

I don't understand
mâi kâo jai   ไม่เข้าใจ

OK
dtòk long   ตกลง

come on, let's go!
bpai gun tèr!   ไปกันเถอะ

what's that in Thai?
pah-săh tai pôot wâh yung-ngai?   ภาษาไทยพูดว่าอย่างไร

could you write it down?
chôo-ay kĕe-un long hâi nòy dâi mái?
                                                 ช่วยเขียนลงให้หน่อยได้ไหม
I don't speak Thai
pôot pah-săh tai mâi bpen   พูดภาษาไทยไม่เป็น

that's fine!
dee láir-o!   ดีแล้ว

พูดไทยเก่ง   **you speak Thai well**
                                poot tai geng

อยู่เมืองไทยนานไหม   **have you been in Thailand long?**
                                yoo meu-ung tai nahn mai?

ไม่เป็นไร   **never mind**
                                mai bpen rai

11

GENERAL PHRASES

เปิด	bpèrt	open
ปิด	bpìt	closed
ชาย	chai	gents
ดึง	deung	pull
ห้าม ...	hâhm ...	.... forbidden
ห้ามสูบบุหรี่	hâhm sòop bOO-rèe	no smoking
ไม่ว่าง	mâi wâhng	engaged
ผลัก	plùk	push
สอบถาม	sòrp tăhm	enquiries
หญิง	yĭng	ladies

COMING AND GOING

airport	sa-nǎhm bin	สนามบิน
baggage	gra-bpǎo	กระเป๋า
book (in advance)	jorng	จอง
bus	rót too-a	รถทัวร์
bus station	sa-tǎh-nee rót may	สถานีรถเมล์
car	rót	รถ
docks	tâh reu-a	ท่าเรือ
ferry	reu-a kâhm fâhk	เรือข้ามฟาก
gate (at airport)	bpra-dtOO	ประตู
harbour	tâh reu-a	ท่าเรือ
plane	krêu-ung bin	เครื่องบิน
sleeper	rót norn	รถนอน
station (train)	sa-tǎh-nee rót fai	สถานีรถไฟ
taxi	táirk-sêe	แท็กซี่
train	rót fai	รถไฟ
tuk-tuk	dtÓOk-dtÓOk	ตุ๊ก ๆ

COMING AND GOING

a ticket to ...
dtŏo-a bpai ...   ตั๋วไป ...

I'd like to reserve a seat
kŏr jorng têe nûng   ขอจองที่นั่ง

smoking/non-smoking please
sòop bOO-rèe dâi/hâhm sòop
   bOO-rèe   สูบบุหรี่ได้/ห้ามสูบบุหรี่

a window seat please
kŏr têe-nûng glâi nâh-dtàhng   ขอที่นั่งใกล้หน้าต่าง

which platform is it for ...?
chahn chah-lah bpai ... yòo
   têe năi?   ชานชาลาไป ... อยู่ที่ไหน

what time is the next flight?
têe-o bin nâh òrk gèe mohng?   เที่ยวบินหน้าออกกี่โมง

is this the right train for ...?
rót fai ka-boo-un née bpai ...
   châi mái?   รถไฟขบวนนี้ไป ... ใช่ไหม

is this bus going to ...?
rót née bpai ... châi mái?   รถนี้ไป ... ใช่ไหม

is this seat free?
têe nûng née wâhng réu bplào?   ที่นั่งนี้ว่างหรือเปล่า

do I have to change (trains)?
dtôrng bplèe-un rót fai réu
   bplào?   ต้องเปลี่ยนรถไฟหรือเปล่า

is this the right stop for ...?
bpai ... dtôrng long têe-nêe réu
   bplào?   ไป ... ต้องลงที่นี่หรือเปล่า

which bus station is it for ...?
bpai ... kêun rót têe sa-tăh-nee
   a-rai?   ไป ... ขึ้นรถที่สถานีอะไร

COMING AND GOING

is this ticket ok?
dtǒo-a bai née chái dâi mái? ตั๋วใบนี้ใช้ได้ไหม

can I change my ticket?
kǒr bplèe-un dtǒo-a dâi mái? ขอเปลี่ยนตั๋วได้ไหม

thanks for a lovely stay
kòrp-kOOn têe ÒOt-sàh doo lair ขอบคุณที่อุตส่าห์ดูแล

thanks very much for coming to meet me
kòrp-kOOn mâhk têe mah rúp ขอบคุณมากที่มารับ

well, here we are in ...
nêe ngai la, mah těung ... láir-o นี่ไงละ มาถึง ... แล้ว

mee a-rai dtôrng sa-dairng mái?
anything to declare? มีอะไรต้องแสดงไหม

chôo-ay bpèrt gra-bpǎo bai née nòy
would you mind opening this
   bag please? ช่วยเปิดกระเป๋าใบนี้หน่อย

ประชาสัมพันธ์	bpra-chah sǎm-pun	information
ชาย	chai	gents
ห้ามสูบบุหรี่	hâhm sòop bOO-rèe	no smoking
ออก	òrk	leaves
ทางออก	tahng òrk	way out
ที่จำหน่ายตั๋ว	têe jum-nài dtǒo-a	ticket office
ถึง	těung	arrives
เวลา	way-lah	time
หญิง	yǐng	ladies

15

air-conditioned room	hôrng dtìt air	ห้องติดแอร์
air-conditioner	krêu-ung air	เครื่องแอร์
bed	dtee-ung	เตียง
breakfast	ah-hăhn cháo	อาหารเช้า
café	kòrp-fêe chórp	คอฟฟี่ช็อบ
dinner	ah-hăhn yen	อาหารเย็น
double room	hôrng kôo	ห้องคู่
guesthouse	gàyt háot	เกสท์เฮาส์
hotel	rohng rairm	โรงแรม
key	gOOn-jair	กุญแจ
lunch	ah-hăhn glahng wun	อาหารกลางวัน
night	keun	คืน
reception	pa-nàirk dtôrn rúp	แผนกต้อนรับ
room	hôrng	ห้อง
shower	fùk boo-a	ฝักบัว
single room	hôrng dèe-o	ห้องเดี่ยว

do you have a room for one night?
mee hôrng wâhng sŭm-rùp
   keun nèung mái?   มีห้องว่างสำหรับคืนหนึ่งไหม

do you have a room for one person?
mee hôrng wâhng sŭm-rùp
   kon dee-o mái?   มีห้องว่างสำหรับคนเดียวไหม

GETTING A ROOM

do you have a room for two people?
mee hôrng wâhng sǔm-rùp
   sòrng kon mái?　　　มีห้องว่างสำหรับสองคนไหม

we'd like to rent a room for a week
rao yàhk ja châo hôrng ah-tít
   nèung　　　เราอยากจะเช่าห้องอาทิตย์หนึ่ง

I'm looking for a good cheap room
dtôrng-gahn hôrng dee-dee têe
   mâi kôy pairng　　　ต้องการห้องดีๆที่ไม่ค่อยแพง

I have a reservation
jorng hôrng wái láir-o　　　จองห้องไว้แล้ว

how much does the room cost?
kâh châo hôrng tâo-rài?　　　คาเช่าห้องเท่าไร

can I see the room please?
kǒr doo hôrng dâi mái?　　　ขอดูห้องได้ไหม

we'd like to stay another night
rao yàhk ja yòo èek keun nèung　　　เราอยากจะอยู่อีกคืนหนึ่ง

we will be arriving late
rao ja mah těung yen-yen nòy　　　เราจะมาถึงเย็นๆหน่อย

can I have my bill please?
kǒr bin nòy dâi mái?　　　ขอบิลหน่อยได้ไหม

I'll pay cash
ja jài bpen ngern sòt　　　จะจ่ายเป็นเงินสด

can I pay by credit card?
kǒr chái bùt kray-dìt jài dâi mái?　　　ขอใช้บัตรเครดิตจ่ายได้ไหม

will you give me a call at 6 in the morning?
chôo-ay rêe-uk pǒm (dee-chún)
   way-lah hòk mohng cháo　　　ช่วยเรียกผม (ดิฉัน) เวลาหกโมงเช้า

17

GETTING A ROOM

can we have breakfast in our room?
sùng ah-hǎhn cháo gin nại
    hôrng dâi mái?   สั่งอาหารเช้ากินในห้องได้ไหม

thanks for putting us up
kòrp-kOOn têe hâi rao mah
    púk yòo dôo-ay   ขอบคุณที่ให้เรามาพักอยู่ด้วย

ชาย	chai	men
เกสท์เฮาส์	gàyt háot	guest house
ห้องให้เช่า	hôrng hâi châo	rooms to let
ห้องน้ำ	hôrng náhm	toilets
ห้องว่าง	hôrng wâhng	vacant room(s)
คอฟฟี่ช็อบ	kòrp-fêe chórp	café serving coffees, alcoholic drinks, snacks and meals
ลิฟท์	líf	lift
สุขา	sÒO-kǎh	toilet
ทางออก	tahng òrk	exit
หญิง	yǐng	ladies

bill	bin	บิล
bowl	chahm	ชาม
chopsticks	dta-gèe-up	ตะเกียบ
dessert	kŏrng wǎhn	ของหวาน
drink *(noun)*	krêu-ung dèum	เครื่องดื่ม
drink *(verb)*	dèum	ดื่ม
eat	gin	กิน
food	ah-hǎhn	อาหาร
menu	may-noo	เมนู
restaurant	ráhn ah-hǎhn	ร้านอาหาร
salad	sa-lùt	สลัด
service	bor-ri-gahn	บริการ
tip	ngern típ	เงินทิป
waiter	kon sèrp	คนเสริฟ
waitress	kon sèrp	คนเสริฟ

EATING OUT

a table for three, please
kŏr dtó sǔm-rùp sǎhm kon
ขอโต๊ะสำหรับสามคน

waiter/waitress!
kOOn krúp (kâ)!
คุณครับ (คะ)

can I see the menu?
kŏr doo may-noo nòy
ขอดูเมนูหน่อย

what do you recommend?
kOOn ja náir-num a-rai?
คุณจะแนะนำอะไร

is it very hot (spicy)?
pèt mâhk mái?
เผ็ดมากไหม

I can't eat spicy food
tahn pèt mâi bpen
ทานเผ็ดไม่เป็น

I'd like ... please
kŏr ...
ขอ ...

can I have what he's having?
kŏr ao yàhng kŏrng kon née dâi
    mái?
ขอเอาอย่างของคนนี้ได้ไหม

that's for me
nûn kŏrng pǒm (chún)
นั่นของผม (ฉัน)

some more rice, please
ao kâo èek krúp (kâ)
เอาข้าวอีกครับ (คะ)

could we have the bill, please?
kŏr bin nòy
ขอบิลหน่อย

EATING OUT

อาหารทะเล	ah-hăhn ta-lay	**seafood**
ชาย	chai	**gents**
ภัตตาคาร	pút-dtah-kahn	**restaurant**
ร้านอาหาร	ráhn ah-hăhn	**restaurant**
หญิง	yĭng	**ladies**

BASIC MEATS

เป็ด	bpèt duck
ไก่	gài chicken
หมู	mŏo pork
เนื้อ	néu-a beef

BASIC SEAFOODS

ปลา	bplah fish
ปลาหมึก	bplah-mèuk squid
ปู	bpoo crab
กุ้ง	gÔOng shrimp, prawn

RICE AND NOODLES

บะหมี่	ba-mèe egg-noodles
ก๋วยเตี๋ยว	gŏo-ay dtĕe-o rice-flour noodles
ขนมจีน	ka-nŏm jeen Thai vermicelli
ข้าว	kâo rice
ข้าวต้ม	kâo dtôm rice porridge

MENU READER

ข้าวเหนียว	kâo nĕe-o
	sticky rice
ข้าวผัด	kâo pùt
	fried rice
ข้าวสวย	kâo sŏo-ay
	boiled rice
หมี่กรอบ	mèe gròrp
	crispy noodles

WAYS OF COOKING AND BASIC COMBINATIONS

... เปรี้ยวหวาน	... bprêe-o wăhn
	sweet and sour ...
... ต้ม	... dtôm
	boiled ...
... อบ	... òp
	oven-cooked ...
... ผัด	... pùt
	stir-fried ...
... ผัดใบกระเพรา	... pùt bai gra-prao
	... fried with basil leaves
... ผัดขิง	... pùt kĭng
	... fried with ginger
... ผัดหน่อไม้	... pùt nòr-mái
	... fried with bamboo shoots
... ผัดพริก	... pùt prík
	... fried with chillies
... ทอด	... tôrt
	deep-fried ...
... ทอดกระเทียมพริกไทย	.. tôrt gra-tee-um prík tai
	... fried with garlic and pepper
... ย่าง	... yâhng
	charcoal-grilled ...

BASIC MEALS

บะหมี่แห้ง	ba-mèe hâirng 'dry' egg noodles (*i.e. without soup*)
บะหมี่น้ำ	ba-mèe náhm egg noodle soup
ก๋วยเตี๋ยวแห้ง	gŏo-ay dtĕe-o hâirng 'dry' noodles (*i.e. without soup*)
ก๋วยเตี๋ยวน้ำ	gŏo-ay dtĕe-o náhm noodle soup
ขนมจีนแกงไก่	ka-nŏm jeen gairng gài Thai vermicelli with chicken curry
ข้าวคลุกกะปิ	kâo klÓÓk ga-bpì rice fried with shrimp paste and served with sweet pork and shredded omelette
ข้าวหมูแดง	kâo mŏo dairng 'red' pork rice
ข้าวมันไก่	kâo mun gài chicken rice
ข้าวหน้าเป็ด	kâo nâh bpèt duck rice
ข้าวผัดปู	kâo pùt bpoo crab fried rice
ข้าวผัดไก่	kâo pùt gài chicken fried rice
ข้าวผัดกุ้ง	kâo pùt gÔÔng shrimp fried rice
ข้าวผัดหมู	kâo pùt mŏo pork fried rice
ผัดราดหน้า	gŏo-ay dtĕe-o pùt râht nâh noodles served with fried meat and vegetables in thick gravy

MENU READER

ผัดซีอิ๊ว
    pùt see éw
    noodles fried in soy sauce

ผัดไทย
    pùt tai
    Thai-style fried noodles

SOUPS AND CURRIES

ต้มยำโป๊ะแตก
    dtôm yum bpó dtàirk
    mixed seafood tom yam
      (spicy soup)

ต้มยำไก่
    dtôm yum gài
    chicken tom yam *(spicy soup)*

ต้มยำกุ้ง
    dtôm yum gÔOng
    shrimp tom yam *(spicy soup)*

แกงไก่
    gairng gài
    chicken curry

แกงกะหรี่
    gairng ga-rèe
    Indian-style curry

แกงจืด
    gairng jèut
    vegetable soup or stock

แกงเขียวหวาน
    gairng kěe-o wǎhn
    beef curry in a green sauce

แกงมัสหมั่น
    gairng mút-sa-mùn
    'Muslim' curry *(with beef,*
      potatoes and peanuts)

แกงเนื้อ
    gairng néu-a
    beef curry

แกงส้ม
    gairng sôm
    spicy vegetable soup

พะแนงไก่
    pa-nairng gài
    'dry' chicken curry *(in thick*
      curry sauce)

พะแนงหมู
    pa-nairng mǒo
    'dry' pork curry

MENU READER

พะแนงเนื้อ

pa-nairng néu-a
'dry' beef curry

FISH AND SEAFOOD

ปลาเปรี้ยวหวาน

bplah bprêe-o wăhn
sweet and sour fish

ปลาหมึกผัดพริก

bplah-mèuk pùt prík
squid fried with chillies

ปลาหมึกทอดกระเทียมพริกไทย

bplah-mèuk tôrt gra-tee-um
prík tai
squid fried with garlic
and pepper

กุ้งผัดใบกระเพรา

gÔOng pùt bai gra-prao
shrimp fried with basil leaves

กุ้งผัดพริก

gÔOng pùt prík
shrimp fried with chillies

กุ้งทอดกระเทียมพริกไทย

gÔOng tôrt gra-tee-um prík tai
prawns fried with garlic
and pepper

BEEF AND CHICKEN DISHES

ไก่ผัดใบกระเพรา

gài pùt bai gra-prao
chicken fried with basil leaves

ไก่ผัดขิง

gài pùt kĭng
chicken fried with ginger

ไก่ผัดเม็ดมะม่วงหิมพานต์

gài pùt mét ma-môo-ung
hĭm-ma-pahn
chicken fried with cashew nuts

ไก่ผัดหน่อไม้

gài pùt nòr-mái
chicken fried with bamboo
shoots

ไก่ผัดหน่อไม้ฝรั่ง

gài pùt nòr-mái fa-rùng
chicken with asparagus

MENU READER

ไก่ผัดพริก
gài pùt prík
chicken fried with chillies

ไก่ทอดกระเทียมพริกไทย
gài tôrt gra-tee-um prík tai
chicken fried with garlic
and pepper

ไก่ย่าง
gài yâhng
roast or barbecued chicken

เนื้อผัดกระเทียมพริกไทย
néu-a pùt gra-tee-um prík tai
beef fried with garlic
and pepper

เนื้อผัดขิง
néu-a pùt kǐng
beef fried with ginger

เนื้อผัดน้ำมันหอย
néu-a pùt núm mun hǒy
beef fried in oyster sauce

เนื้อสับผัดพริกกระเพรา
néu-a sùp pùt prík gra-prao
minced beef fried with
chillies and basil

PORK AND DUCK DISHES

เป็ดย่าง
bpèt yâhng
roast duck

หมูเปรี้ยวหวาน
mǒo bprêe-o wǎhn
sweet and sour pork

หมูผัดขิง
mǒo pùt kǐng
pork fried with ginger

หมูผัดพริก
mǒo pùt prík
pork fried with chillies

หมูสับผัดพริกกระเพรา
mǒo sùp pùt prík gra-prao
minced pork fried with
chillies and basil

หมูทอดกระเทียมพริกไทย
mǒo tôrt gra-tee-um prík tai
pork fried with garlic
and pepper

MISCELLANEOUS DISHES

ปอเปี้ยะทอด	bpor bpêe-a tôrt Thai spring roll
ไข่ดาว	kài dao fried egg
ไข่เจียว	kài jee-o omelette
ไข่ลูกเขย	kài lôok kěr-ee 'son-in-law' eggs (hard-boiled eggs garnished with various condiments)
ไข่พะโล้	kài pa-lóh egg stewed in soy sauce and spices
ไข่ยัดไส้	kài yút sâi filled omelette
ขนมจีบ	ka-nŏm jèep dim-sum (balls of minced pork in dough)
หมูสะเต๊ะ	mŏo sa-dtáy pork satay (thin strips of pork, charcoal-grilled, served with sauce)
ส้มตำ	sôm dtum papaya salad made with unripe papaya
ทอดมัน	tôrt mun deep-fried fish-cakes

MENU READER

VEGETABLES

แตงกวา	dtairng-gwah cucumber
ต้นหอม	dtôn hǒrm spring onion
กระหล่ำปลี	gra-lùm-bplee cabbage
กระเทียม	gra-tee-um garlic
เห็ด	hèt mushroom
หัวหอม	hǒo-a hǒrm onion
ข้าวโพด	kâo pôht sweet corn
ขิง	kǐng ginger
มะเขือเทศ	ma-kěu-a tâyt tomato
หน่อไม้	nòr mái bamboo shoots
พริก	prík chilli
ผัก	pùk vegetable
ผักบุ้ง	pùk bôÔng morning glory (green leafy vegetable)
ผักคะน้า	pùk ka-náh spring greens

MENU READER

ถั่วลันเตา

tòo-a lun-dtao
mange-tout

ถั่วงอก

tòo-a ngôrk
bean sprouts

DESSERTS

กล้วยบวชชี

glôo-ay bòo-ut chee
banana served in very sweet
   coconut milk sauce

ตะโก้

dta-gôh
Thai-style jelly covered with a
   thick layer of coconut cream

ข้าวเหนียวมะม่วง

kǎo něe-o ma-mǒo-ung
sweet sticky rice and mango
   topped with coconut cream

FRUIT

ชมพู่

chom-pôo
rose apple (shaped like large
   strawberry - red, pink or white)

แตงโม

dtairng moh
water melon

ฝรั่ง

fa-rùng
guava (green skin with
   pinkish-white flesh)

กล้วย

glôo-ay
banana

ขนุน

ka-nǒOn
jackfruit (melon-shaped with
   green skin and yellow flesh)

ละมุด

la-mÓOt
sapodilla (small brown fruit,
   similar taste to pear)

ลิ้นจี่	lín-jèe lychee
ลำใย	lum-yai longan (similar to lychee)

มะละกอ	ma-la-gor
	papaya (oblong shape with
	    yellow skin and soft
	    orange flesh)

มะม่วง	ma-môo-ung mango
มะพร้าว	ma-práo coconut
เงาะ	ngór rambutan (small with reddish prickly skin and white flesh)
น้อยหน่า	nóy-nàh custard apple (heart-shaped with green skin and white flesh)
ผลไม้	pŏn-la-mái fruit
ส้ม	sôm orange
ส้มโอ	sôm oh pomelo (similar to grapefruit)
สับปะรด	sùp-bpa-rót pineapple

ทุเรียน	tOO-ree-un
	durian (very large fruit with
	    green spiky skin, yellow
	    flesh and a pungent smell)

HAVING A DRINK

bar	bah	บาร์
beer	bee-a	เบียร์
coconut juice	núm ma-práo	น้ำมะพร้าว
coke*	kóhk	โค้ก
fresh orange	núm sôm kún	น้ำส้มคั้น
ice	núm kǎirng	น้ำแข็ง
lemonade	núm ma-nao	น้ำมะนาว
soda water	núm soh-dah	น้ำโซดา
whisky	wít-sa-gêe	วิสกี้

let's go for a drink
bpai hǎh a-rai dèum gun nòy ไปหาอะไรดื่มกันหน่อย

a beer please
kǒr bee-a kòo-ut nèung ขอเบียร์ขวดหนึ่ง

two beers please
kǒr bee-a sǒrng kòo-ut ขอเบียร์สองขวด

with lots of ice
sài núm kǎirng yér yáir ใส่น้ำแข็งเยอะแยะ

no ice thanks
mâi sài núm kǎirng ไม่ใส่น้ำแข็ง

the same again please *(drinks
    served in bottles)*
kǒr èek kòo-ut ขออีกขวด

32

HAVING A DRINK

the same again please *(drinks served in glasses)*
kŏr èek gâir-o   ขออีกแก้ว

what'll you have?
ja dèum a-rai?   จะดื่มอะไร

not for me thanks
pŏm (chún) mâi ao   ผม (ฉัน) ไม่เอา

he's absolutely smashed
káo mao ǎirn   เขาเมาแอ๋น

เบียร์สิงห์	bee-a sǐng	Singha® beer *(type of lager)*
บริการ ๒๔ ชั่วโมง	bor-ri-gahn yêe-sìp sèe chôo-a mohng	24 hour service
คอฟฟี่ช็อบ	kòrp-fêe chórp	café serving coffees, alcoholic drinks and meals
แม่โขง	mâir-kǒhng	Mekhong® whisky *(strong local whisky)*

that's crazy!
bâh!
บ้า

it's great fun
sa-nÒOk dee
สนุกดี

it's a real hassle
yâir jung ler-ee
แย่จังเลย

I'm fed up
bèu-a
เบื่อ

I'm absolutely knackered
nèu-ay ja dtai
เหนื่อยจะตาย

it's fantastic
dee mâhk ler-ee
ดีมากเลย

it's a rip-off
tum-mai tĕung pairng
   yung ngún?
ทำไมถึงแพงอย่างนั้น

this heat's killing me
rórn ja dtai
ร้อนจะตาย

ฝรั่ง
fa-rùng
foreigner (Westerner)

พี่
pêe
'older brother/sister' (a friendly
   and polite way of addressing
   people a little older than oneself)

34

bike	jùk-gra-yahn	จักรยาน
bus	rót may	รถเมล์
car	rót yon	รถยนต์
change (*trains*)	bplèe-un	เปลี่ยน
garage (*for fuel*)	bpúm núm mun	ปั๊มน้ำมัน
map	păirn-têe	แผนที่
motorbike	rót mor-dter-sai	รถมอเตอร์ไซค์
petrol	núm mun	น้ำมัน
return (ticket)	dtŏo-a bpai glùp	ตั๋วไปกลับ
single (ticket)	dtŏo-a bpai têe-o dee-o	ตั๋วไปเที่ยวเดียว
station	sa-ăh-nee rót fai	สถานีรถไฟ
taxi	táirk-sêe	แท็กซี่
ticket	dtŏo-a	ตั๋ว
train	rót fai	รถไฟ
tuk-tuk	dtÓOk-dtÓOk	ตุ๊กๆ

I'd like to rent a motorbike/car
yàhk ja châo rót mor-dter-sai/
   rót yon

อยากจะเช่ารถมอร์เตอร์ไซค์/รถยนต์

how much is it per day?
wun la tâo-rài?

วันละเท่าไร

**when do I have to bring the
   motorbike back?**
ja dtôrng ao rót mor-dter-sai
   mah keun mêu-rai?

จะต้องเอารถมอร์เตอร์ไซค์มาคืนเมื่อไร

I'm heading for ...
bpai ...

ไป ...

GETTING AROUND

how do I get to ...?
bpai ... bpai tahng năi?

ไป ... ไปทางไหน

REPLIES

ตรงไปเลย
dtrong bpai ler-ee
straight on

เลี้ยวซ้าย/ขวา
lée-o sái/kwăh
turn left/right

ตึกหลังโน้นไงล่ะ
dtèuk lŭng nóhn ngai lâ
it's that building there

ต้องกลับไปทางเก่า
dtôrng glùp bpai tahng gào
it's back that way

เลี้ยวซ้ายทางแยกที่หนึ่ง/
ที่สอง/ที่สาม
lée-o sái tahng yâirk têe nèung/
têe sŏrng/têe săhm
first/second/third on the left

เรามาเที่ยวครับ (ค่ะ)
we're just travelling around
rao mah têe-o krúp (kâ)

จะผ่านหรือเปล่า
is that on the way?
ja pàhn réu bplào?

จะลงที่นี่ได้ไหม
can I get off here?
ja long têe-nêe dâi mái?

ขอบคุณมากที่มาส่ง
thanks very much for the lift
kòrp-kOOn mâhk têe mah sòng

36

GETTING AROUND

two returns to ... please
kŏr dtŏo-a bpai glùp
   ... sŏrng bai
ขอตั๋วไปกลับ ... สองใบ

what time is the last bus back to ...?
rót may glùp ... têe-o sÕÕt
   tái òrk gèe mohng?
รถเมล์กลับ ... เที่ยวสุดท้ายออกกี่โมง

we want to leave tomorrow and come back the day after
rao yàhk ja bpai prÕÕng née
   láir-o glùp ma-reun née
เราอยากจะไปพรุ่งนี้แล้วกลับมะรืนนี้

we're coming back the same day
rao ja glùp mah wun
   dee-o gun
เราจะกลับมาวันเดียวกัน

is this the right platform for ...?
têe-née bpen chahn chah-lah
   bpai ... réu bplào?
ที่นี่เป็นชานชาลาไป ... หรือเปล่า

is this bus going to ...?
rót née bpai ... châi mái
รถนี้ไป ... ใช่ไหม

where are we?
rao tĕung năi láir-o?
เราถึงไหนแล้ว

which stop is it for ...?
bpai ... dtôrng long têe-năi?
ไป ... ต้องลงที่ไหน

how far is it to the nearest petrol station?
bpúm núm mun têe glâi têe
   sÕÕt yòo têe năi?
ปั๊มน้ำมันที่ใกล้ที่สุดอยู่ที่ไหน

I need a new tyre
dtôrng-gahn yahng mài
ต้องการยางใหม่

it's overheating
krêu-ung yon rórn
เครื่องยนต์ร้อน

there's something wrong with
   the brakes
bràyk mâi kôy dee
เบรคไม่ค่อยดี

37

GETTING AROUND

อะไหล่	a-lài	spares
บริการ ๒๔ ช.ม.	bor-ri-gahn yêe-sìp sèe chôo-a mohng	24 hour service
ปะยาง	bpà yahng	punctures repaired
ประชาสัมพันธ์	bpra-chah sǔm-pun	information
ห้ามจอดรถ	hâhm jòrt rót	no parking
ห้ามเข้า	hâhm kâo	no entry
ห้ามสูบบุหรี่	hâhm sòop bOO-rèe	no smoking
อู่	òo	garage
ออก	òrk	departs
ที่จำหน่ายตั๋ว	têe jum-nài dtǒo-a	ticket office
ถึง	tǔeng	arrives

carrier bag	tǒOng gra-dàht	ถุงกระดาษ
cashdesk	têe jài ngern sòt	ที่จ่ายเงินสด
cheap	tòok	ถูก
cheque	chék	เช็ค
department	pa-nàirk	แผนก
expensive	pairng	แพง
market	dta-làht	ตลาด
pay	jài	จ่าย
receipt	bai sèt rúp ngern	ใบเสร็จรับเงิน
shop	ráhn	ร้าน
shop assistant	pa-núk ngahn kǎi	พนักงานขาย
supermarket	sǒOp-bpêr-mah-gèt	ซุปเปอร์มาร์เก็ต

I'd like ...
dtôrng-gahn ...   ต้องการ ...

have you got ...?
mee ... mái?   มี ... ไหม

how much is this?
nêe tâo-rài?   นี่เท่าไร

could you lower the
  price a little?
lót rah-kah nòy dâi mái?   ลดราคาหน่อยได้ไหม

that's too expensive
pairng gern bpai   แพงเกินไป

how about ... baht?
... bàht dâi mái?   ... บาทได้ไหม

SHOPPING

do you take credit cards?
rúp bùt kray-dìt réu bplào?　　　รับบัตรเครดิตหรือเปล่า

could I have a receipt please?
kŏr bai sèt rúp ngern dôo-ay　　　ขอใบเสร็จรับเงินด้วย

I'd like to try it on
kŏr lorng sài doo dâi mái?　　　ขอลองใส่ดูได้ไหม

it's too big/small
yài/lék gern bpai　　　ใหญ่/เล็กเกินไป

it's not what I'm looking for
mâi châi têe pŏm (chún)
　　dtôrng-gahn　　　ไม่ใช่ที่ผม (ฉัน) ต้องการ

I'll take it
ao un née　　　เอาอันนี้

can you gift-wrap it?
chôo-ay hòr kŏrng kwŭn
　　hâi nòy dâi mái?　　　ช่วยห่อของขวัญให้หน่อยได้ไหม

ต้องการอะไรครับ (คะ)　　　dtôrng gahn a-rai krúp (ká)?
can I help you?

ไม่มีครับ (ค่ะ)　　　mâi mee krúp (kâ)
we don't have any

ขายหมดครับ (ค่ะ)　　　kăi mòt krúp (kâ)
we've sold out

40

SHOPPING

บาท	bàht	baht *(unit of currency)*
เปิด	bpèrt	open
ปิด	bpìt	closed
ลดราคา	lót rah-kah	sale/reduced
ราคา	rah-kah	price
ทางเข้า	tahng kâo	entry
ทางออก	tahng òrk	exit

FESTIVALS

Songkran
This is the Thai New Year which occurs in mid-April. Over the years it has developed into an occasion where people throw water at one another as a form of friendly greeting.

Loy Kratong
This takes place in November on the night of the full moon. Thais will take their 'kratong' - a lotus-shaped boat containing a lighted candle, incense sticks and often a coin - and place them in the river or canal to honour the water spirits and wash away their sins.

RELIGION

The vast majority of Thais are Buddhists. For most Thai men this means spending a period - traditionally about three months but nowadays often as little as a week - living in a temple as a monk. Thais are generally very relaxed and extremely tolerant about religious practices. The visitor should, however, treat Buddha images, monks and temples with respect and observe any regulations concerning these. Some city temples will refuse admission to foreigners casually dressed in shorts and beach sandals. When visiting a temple, it is important to be aware that in some parts everyone removes their shoes; there may be a notice prohibiting photographs in some places and it is good manners if in doubt to ask an official. Taking Buddha images out of the country without the necessary documentation is also forbidden so it is wise to check up on the regulations very carefully before making any purchases. Female visitors should take care to avoid any close physical contact with monks, for example sitting on the next seat on a bus; Thais, both men and women, will always give up their seats to a monk and women will usually move some distance down the bus.

THAILAND AND THINGS THAI

THE MONARCHY

The monarchy is regarded with deep respect by Thais and pictures of the King and royal family are to be found in most Thai homes. Negative comments about the royal family - especially from foreigners - are liable to cause deep offence to the average Thai and can lead to more serious trouble. Since the overthrow of the absolute monarchy in 1932, and its replacement by a constitutional monarchy, Thailand has aspired to a democratic system of government. For much of the time, however, the country has been run by a military government or a civilian government that depended on military support for its survival. Military coups, usually bloodless, continue to be - even in the 1990s - a recurring pattern in modern Thai politics.

GETTING AROUND

You can travel around Bangkok by ordinary bus, air-conditioned bus, 'samlor' (three-wheeler motorized pedi-cab) or taxi. Excellent maps indicating the various bus routes can be purchased from bookstores and hotels. If you are planning to go by 'samlor' or taxi then be prepared to bargain over the price before stepping into the vehicle - try offering a suitable amount: '... bàht dâi mái?' (how about .. baht?). A number of bus companies run regular, cheap, air-conditioned bus services to provinces outside Bangkok; it's usually necessary to book a day or two in advance. Hiring a car is another way of getting around but in Bangkok, at least, it is not to be recommended because of the chaotic traffic conditions; it's probably cheaper and certainly less stressful to use taxis. It's often possible to hire motorcycles in provincial towns and popular resorts; although the climate makes this an ideal way of travelling around, this is best left to the experienced rider able to assess the road-worthiness of the hired vehicle.

THAILAND AND THINGS THAI

SIGHTSEEING

Traditionally, tourists have tended to divide their time between Bangkok, Chiangmai in the north and Pattaya, a coastal resort some 2 hours drive to the east of Bangkok.

Bangkok

In and around Bangkok, among the most popular destinations are temples such as 'Wat Pra Kaeo' (the Temple of the Emerald Buddha), 'Wat Po' and 'Wat Arun' (the Temple of Dawn), the National Museum, the 'dta-làht náhm' (floating market) and the Thai classical dance performances staged in certain restaurants.

Chiangmai

The climate here is a little cooler than Bangkok and most tourists take the opportunity to visit one of the hill-tribe villages outside the city. It's even possible to go on organised treks involving an overnight stay in a hill-tribe village.

The tourist industry has grown enormously in the last decade or so and once remote provinces such as Mae Hong Sorn near the Burmese border and Nakhon Phanom on the border with Laos now regularly play host to the more adventurous traveller. Good transport services between provinces and a variety of extremely informative Western-language guide books make it relatively easy even for the non-Thai speaker to see a large part of the country.

NIGHT LIFE

The bars of Bangkok's Patpong Road and the massage parlours that became popular during the American military presence in Indo-China have earned the city a certain notoriety for its night life. They continue to be popular with both foreign tourists and Thai men despite the potentially huge Aids crisis that experts predict will occur in Thailand. The most popular night time 'entertainment' for most

THAILAND AND THINGS THAI

people in Thailand, however, is eating out: there are restaurants and coffee shops to suit every taste and almost every income, some specialising in certain regional cuisines and others offering live musical entertainment. Discos have become more numerous in the big cities in recent years, while nightclubs with live music are popular in the smaller provincial towns.

SHOPPING

Although not appropriate in large department stores, you should certainly haggle over the price when shopping in markets, at pavement stalls and in warehouses selling silk and jewellery. Whenever bargaining, however, whether with taxi drivers or street vendors, always do so in a good tempered manner; an aggressive approach, or treating the vendor as if he is a cheat and swindler will neither help to seal the deal nor impress anyone very much.

In small shops, even where there are prices displayed on goods, it is sometimes possible to negotiate a small - often token - discount; you can enquire by asking 'ja lòt nòy dâi mái?' (can you lower the price a little?). Thai silk is a favourite with foreign shoppers and local tailors and dressmakers will make up garments within a couple of days at a very reasonable price.

ADDRESSING PEOPLE

When addressing Thais, use the polite title *Khun* 'kOOn' in front of the first name, regardless of whether it is a male or female that you are speaking to. Surnames are never used when addressing someone.

GESTURES

Certain gestures which are acceptable in one country can often cause offence in another. In Thailand, pointing at something with your foot, pointing your foot at someone and sitting with your feet on a desk are all considered extremely bad manners. Touching somebody on the head or ruffling someone's hair are also offensive to Thais.

DRESS

Appearances are extremely important in Thailand and Thais take great care over the way they dress. For the Westerner, it is probably advisable to dress on the conservative side, especially if visiting Thais, accompanying them on outings, and visiting temples; some temples in fact display notices warning that tourists 'impolitely dressed' will not be admitted and you do not have to be particularly observant to notice the disapproving looks from Thais at some of the foreigners wandering around their country!

VISITING A HOME

If you visit a Thai home, it is customary to take off your shoes before entering the house. It is appropriate to greet people who are of a similar age or older with a 'wai', holding the hands in a prayer-like position in front of the forehead; they will probably respond in a similar manner, while you should wait for younger members of the household to 'wai' you before responding.

EATING

A Thai meal normally consists of plain boiled rice accompanied by a variety of main dishes. Thais eat with a spoon and fork - not chopsticks (unless eating noodles in a Chinese noodle shop). When eating Thai food you should take a small amount from one or more of the main dishes and eat it with some rice on your plate; when this is finished, help yourself to some more, either from the same main dish or from another. If you are eating with a Thai, he or she will almost certainly want to ask you, 'a-ròy mái?' (is it nice?) to which you will probably want to reply, 'a-ròy' (yes). Another favourite question to ask 'farang'

THAILAND AND THINGS THAI

(Westerners) is 'pèt mái?' (is it hot/spicy?), and if your host has clearly gone to great lengths to order something that will not leave you feeling your tongue has been singed it is only diplomatic to reply, 'mâi pèt' (no).

THAI WRITING

Thai is written in an alphabetic script which had its origins in South India. Although unique, it bears a close resemblance to the Lao and Cambodian scripts. Thai is written across the page from left to right. Spaces do not appear between words but are used as punctuation marks, corresponding roughly to the Western use of commas and full stops. Vowel symbols can be written after a consonant, in front of it, above it and below it - or even surrounding it on three sides.

ม	–า	มา	(come)
m	-ah	mah	
ใ–	น	ใน	(in)
-ai	n	nai	
◌ี	ด	ดี	(good)
-ee	d	dee	
◌ู	ด	ดู	(look)
-oo	d	doo	
เ–ีย	ม	เมีย	(wife)
-ee-a	m	mee-a	

THAILAND AND THINGS THAI

THAI DIALECTS

Different dialects are spoken in different regions of Thailand and Thais from Bangkok will probably have difficulty understanding the local dialects spoken in the North, the North-east and the South. In schools throughout the country, however, the Central Thai dialect is used as the language of instruction and virtually all Thais will speak this in addition to their own local dialect. With a large number of different ethnic and linguistic groups living in the country, it is by no means unusual to come across Thais who are fluent in several different languages and dialects.

THAI CALENDAR

The Buddhist Era (B.E.), rather than A.D. is often used for expressing the year in Thailand. To convert the A.D. year to B.E. simply add 543. Thus, 1990 A.D. becomes 2533 in the Buddhist Era.

baht (national currency)	bàht	บาท
bank	ta-nah-kahn	ธนาคาร
bill	bin	บิล
bureau de change	têe lâirk bplèe-un ngern	ที่แลกเปลี่ยนเงิน
change (small)	sàyt ngern	เศษเงิน
cheque	chék	เช็ค
credit card	bùt kray-dìt	บัตรเครดิต
expensive	pairng	แพง
pounds (sterling)	ngern bporn	เงินปอนด์
price	rah-kah	ราคา
receipt	bai sèt rúp ngern	ใบเสร็จรับเงิน
traveller's cheque	chék dern tahng	เช็คเดินทาง

how much is it?
tâo-rài?   เท่าไร

I'd like to change this into ...
yàhk ja lâirk bplèe-un bpen ...   อยากจะแลกเปลี่ยนเป็น ...

can you give me something smaller?
kŏr báirng yôy dâi mái?   ขอแบ๊งค์ย่อยได้ไหม

can I use this credit card?
bùt kray-dìt née chái dâi mái?   บัตรเครดิตนี้ใช้ได้ไหม

can we have the bill please?
kŏr bin krúp (kâ)   ขอบิลครับ (ค่ะ)

please keep the change
mâi dtôrng torn ròrk   ไม่ต้องทอนหรอก

MONEY

does that include service?
roo-um kâh bor-ri-gahn
  réu bplào?

รวมค่าบริการหรือเปล่า

I think the figures are wrong
kít wâh kít ngern pìt

คิดว่าคิดเงินผิด

I'm completely skint
ngern mòt dtoo-a láir-o

เงินหมดตัวแล้ว

The unit is the 'baht' which is divided into 100 'satang'. Coin denominations are: 5, 2 and 1 baht; 50 and 25 satang. Notes are: 500 baht (purple), 100 (red), 50 (blue), 20 (green) and 10 (brown).

บาท	bàht	baht
แลกเปลี่ยนเงินตราต่างประเทศ	lâirk bplèe-un ngern dtrah dtàhng bpra-tâyt	bureau de change
ธนาคาร	ta-nah-kahn	bank
อัตราแลกเปลี่ยนเงินตราต่างประเทศ	ùt-dtrah lâirk bplèe-un ngern dtrah dtàhng bpra-tâyt	exchange rate

band *(pop)*	wong don-dtree	วงดนตรี
cinema	rohng nǔng	โรงหนัง
concert	korn-sèrt	คอนเสิร์ต
disco	dit-sa-gôh	ดิสโก้
film	nǔng	หนัง
go out	bpai têe-o	ไปเที่ยว
music	don-dtree	ดนตรี
play *(theatre)*	la-korn	ละคร
seat	têe nûng	ที่นั่ง
show	gahn sa-dairng	การแสดง
singer	núk rórng	นักร้อง
Thai boxing	moo-ay tai	มวยไทย
Thai classical dance	rum tai	รำไทย
theatre	rohng la-korn	โรงละคร
ticket	dtǒo-a	ตั๋ว

are you doing anything tonight?
keun née wâhng réu bplào? คืนนี้ว่างหรือเปล่า

do you want to come out with me tonight?
keun née bpai têe-o dôo-ay
  gun mái? คืนนี้ไปเที่ยวด้วยกันไหม

what's on?
mee a-rai nâh doo bâhng? มีอะไรน่าดูบ้าง

where is there a good disco round here?
tǎir-o née mee dit-sa-gôh dee
  dee têe nǎi bâhng? แถวนี้มีดิสโก้ดีๆที่ไหนบ้าง

51

ENTERTAINMENT

let's go to the cinema
bpai doo nǔng dee mái?　　　　ไปดูหนังดีไหม

I've seen it
bpai doo láir-o　　　　ไปดูแล้ว

I'll meet you at 8 p.m. at the station
póp gun têe sa-tǎh-nee rót fai
　　way-lah sǒrng tÔOm　　　　พบกันที่สถานีรถไฟเวลา ๒ ทุ่ม

two tickets for tonight please
ao dtǒo-a sǒrng bai sǔm-rùp
　　keun née　　　　เอาตั๋วสองใบสำหรับคืนนี้

I'd like to book three seats for tomorrow
yàhk ja jorng dtǒo-a sǎhm bai
　　sǔm-rùp prÔOng née　　　　อยากจะจองตั๋วสามใบสำหรับพรุ่งนี้

do you want to dance?
dtên rum mái?　　　　เต้นรำไหม

do you want to dance again?
dtên rum èek mái?　　　　เต้นรำอีกไหม

thanks but I'm with my boyfriend
kòrp-kOOn kâ dtàir dtorn née
　　mee fairn mah dôo-ay　　　　ขอบคุณค่ะ แต่ตอนนี้มีแฟนมาด้วย

let's go out for some fresh air
òrk bpai kâhng nôrk nòy
　　dee mái?　　　　ออกไปข้างนอกหน่อยดีไหม

will you let me back in again later?
glùp mah láir-o bpèrt bpra-dtoo
　　hâi nòy dâi mái?　　　　กลับมาแล้วเปิดประตูให้หน่อยได้ไหม

I'm meeting someone inside
mee nút gùp kon kâhng nai　　　　มีนัดกับคนข้างใน

อาบอบนวด	àhp òp nôo-ut	massage
บริการ ๒๔ ช.ม.	bor-ri-gahn yêe-sìp sèe chôo-a mohng	24-hour service
ฉายวันนี้	chăi wun née	now showing
เต็ม	dtem	full
ห้ามสูบบุหรี่	hâhm sòop bOO-rèe	no smoking
ไนทคลับ	náit klúp	night club
เร็วๆนี้	ray-o ray-o née	coming soon
รอบ	rôrp	show
สุขา	sÒO-kăh	toilets
สุขาชาย	sÒO-kăh chai	men's toilets
สุขาหญิง	sÒO-kăh yĭng	ladies' toilets
ทางเข้า	tahng kâo	entrance
ทางออก	tahng òrk	exit
ที่จำหน่ายตั๋ว	têe jum-nài dtŏo-a	booking office

beach	chai hàht	ชายหาด
beach umbrella	rôm	ร่ม
bikini	bi-gi-nêe	บิกินี่
dive *(verb)*	gra-dòht náhm	กระโดดน้ำ
sand	sai	ทราย
sea	ta-lay	ทะเล
sunbathe	àhp dàirt	อาบแดด
suntan lotion	kreem tah àhp dàirt	ครีมทาอาบแดด
suntan oil	núm mun tah àhp dàirt	น้ำมันทาอาบแดด
swim *(verb)*	wâi náhm	ว่ายน้ำ
swimming costume	chóOt wâi náhm	ชุดว่ายน้ำ
towel	pâh chét dtoo-a	ผ้าเช็ดตัว
wave	klêun	คลื่น

let's go down to the beach
bpai chai hàht mái?
ไปชายหาดไหม

what's the water like?
náhm bpen yung-ngay?
น้ำเป็นอย่างไร

is it clean?
sa-àht mái?
สะอาดไหม

it's lovely and warm
ÒOn dee jung ler-ee
อุ่นดีจังเลย

are you coming for a swim?
bpai wâi náhm dôo-ay gun mái?
ไปว่ายน้ำด้วยกันไหม

I can't swim
wâi náhm mâi bpen
ว่ายน้ำไม่เป็น

THE BEACH

he swims like a fish
káo wâi náhm měu-un bplah
เขาว่ายน้ำเหมือนปลา

will you keep an eye on my things
  for me?
chôo-ay doo kŏrng hâi nòy dâi mái?
ช่วยดูของให้หน่อยได้ไหม

is it deep here?
náhm têe-nêe léuk mái?
น้ำที่นี่ลึกไหม

I'm all sunburnt
pŏm (chún) tòok dàirt păo
ผม (ฉัน) ถูกแดดเผา

let's go and get something to drink
bpai hăh a-rai dèum gun tèr
ไปหาอะไรดื่มกันเถอะ

do you have beach umbrellas
  for hire?
mee rôm gun dàirt hâi châo mái?
มีร่มกันแดดให้เช่าไหม

55

accident	OO-bùt-dti-hàyt	อุบัติเหตุ
ambulance	rót pa-yah-bahn	รถพยาบาล
broken *(bones)*	hùk	หัก
broken *(things)*	dtàirk	แตก
doctor	mŏr	หมอ
emergency	chÒOk chěrn	ฉุกเฉิน
fire	fai mâi	ไฟไหม้
fire brigade	nòo-ay dùp plerng	หน่วยดับเพลิง
ill	mâi sa-bai	ไม่สบาย
injured	bàht jèp	บาดเจ็บ
late	cháh	ช้า
out of order	sěe-a	เสีย
police	dtum-ròo-ut	ตำรวจ

can you help me? I'm lost
chôo-ay nòy dâi mái? pŏm
 (chún) lŏng tahng

ช่วยหน่อยได้ไหม ผม (ฉัน) หลงทาง

I've lost my passport
núng-sěu dern tahng kŏrng
 pŏm (chún) hăi

หนังสือเดินทางของผม (ฉัน) หาย

I've locked myself out of my room
gOOn-jair yòo kâhng nai kâo
 mâi dâi

กุญแจอยู่ข้างใน เข้าไม่ได้

my luggage hasn't arrived
gra-bpăo kŏrng pŏm (chún)
 yung mâi mah

กระเป๋าของผม (ฉัน) ยังไม่มา

I can't get it open
bpèrt mâi dâi

เปิดไม่ได้

56

PROBLEMS

it's jammed
mun dtìt
มันติด

I don't have enough money
mee ngern mâi por
มีเงินไม่พอ

I've broken down
rót sěe-a
รถเสีย

this is an emergency
nêe bpen rêu-ung chÒOk-chěrn
นี่เป็นเรื่องฉุกเฉิน

help!
chôo-ay dôo-ay!
ช่วยด้วย

it doesn't work
chái mâi dâi
ใช้ไม่ได้

the lights aren't working in
  my room
fai nai hôrng pǒm (chún) sěe-a
ไฟในห้องผม (ฉัน) เสีย

the lift is stuck
líf dtìt
ลิฟท์ติด

I can't understand a single word
mâi kâo jai ler-ee
ไม่เข้าใจเลย

can you get an interpreter?
chôo-ay hǎh kon bplair dâi mái?
ช่วยหาคนแปลได้ไหม

the toilet won't flush
hôrng náhm chúk krôhk mâi dâi
ห้องน้ำชักโครกไม่ได้

there's no plug in the bath
mâi mee bplúk nai àhng àhp
  náhm
ไม่มีปลั๊กในอ่างอาบน้ำ

there's no hot water
mâi mee núm rórn
ไม่มีน้ำร้อน

there's no toilet paper left
mâi mee gra-dàht chum-rá
ไม่มีกระดาษชำระ

PROBLEMS

I'm afraid I've accidentally broken the ...
pŏm (chún) grayng wâh tum ...
  dtàirk doy-ee bung-ern ผม (ฉัน) เกรงว่าทำ ... แตกโดยบังเอิญ

this man has been following me
pôo-chai kon née dtahm
  chún mah ผู้ชายคนนี้ตามฉันมา

I've been mugged
pŏm (chún) tòok jêe ผม (ฉัน) ถูกจี้

my handbag has been stolen
gra-bpăo tĕu korng chún tòok
  ka-moy-ee กระเป๋าถือของฉันถูกขโมย

ตำรวจ	police	dtum-ròo-ut
ห้าม ...	... forbidden	hâhm ...
ห้ามเข้า	no entry	hâhm kâo
ห้ามสูบบุหรี่	no smoking	hâhm sòop bOO-rèe
ระวัง	caution	ra-wung
อันตราย	danger	un-dta-rai

bandage	pâh pun plăir	ผ้าพันแผล
blood	lêu-ut	เลือด
broken *(bones)*	hùk	หัก
burn *(noun)*	plăir mâi	แผลไหม้
chemist's	ráhn kăi yah	ร้านขายยา
contraception	gahn kOOm gum-nèrt	การคุมกำเนิด
dentist	mŏr fun	หมอฟัน
disabled	pí-gahn	พิการ
disease	rôhk	โรค
doctor	mŏr	หมอ
health	sOOk-ka-pâhp	สุขภาพ
hospital	rohng pa-yah-bahn	โรงพยาบาล
ill	mâi sa-bai	ไม่สบาย
nurse	nahng pa-yah-bahn	นางพยาบาล
wound	plăir	แผล

I don't feel well
róo-sèuk mâi sa-bai
รู้สึกไม่สบาย

it's getting worse
yâir long tOOk tee
แย่ลงทุกที

I feel better
róo-sèuk kôy yung chôo-a
รู้สึกค่อยยังชั่ว

I feel sick
róo-sèuk ja ah-jee-un
รู้สึกจะอาเจียน

I've got a pain here
jèp dtrong née
เจ็บตรงนี้

HEALTH

it hurts
jèp

เจ็บ

he's got a high temperature
káo bpen kâi kêun sŏong

เขาเป็นไข้ขึ้นสูง

could you call a doctor?
chôo-ay rêe-uk mŏr hâi nòy
dâi mái?

ช่วยเรียกหมอให้หน่อยได้ไหม

is it serious?
bpen nùk jing jing rěu?

เป็นหนักจริงๆหรือ

will he need an operation?
káo ja dtôrng pàh dtùt réu
bplào?

เขาจะต้องผ่าตัดหรือเปล่า

I'm diabetic
pŏm (chún) bpen rôhk
bao wăhn

ผม (ฉัน) เป็นโรคเบาหวาน

have you got anything for ...?
mee yah gâir ... mái?

มียาแก้ ... ไหม

ตรวจสายตา	eye test	dtròo-ut săi dtah
คลีนิค	clinic	klee-ník
น.พ.	doctor (*male*)	nai pâirt
พ.ญ.	doctor (*female*)	pâirt yĭng
โรงพยาบาล	hospital	rohng pa-yah-bahn
ทำฟัน	dentist's	tum fun

60

(Thai) boxing	moo-ay (tai)	มวย (ไทย)
football	fÓOt-born	ฟุตบอล
golf	górf	กอล์ฟ
golf course	sa-nǎhm górf	สนามกอล์ฟ
play *(verb)*	lên	เล่น
stadium	sa-nǎhm gee-lah	สนามกีฬา
swim *(verb)*	wâi náhm	ว่ายน้ำ
swimming pool	sà wâi náhm	สระว่ายน้ำ
tennis	ten-nít	เทนนิส
tennis court	sa-nǎhm ten-nít	สนามเทนนิส
water-skiing	lên sa-gee náhm	เล่นสกีน้ำ

**I would like to learn to
  waterski**
yàhk ja ree-un lên sa-gee náhm   อยากจะเรียนเล่นสกีน้ำ

I would like to hire ...
yàhk ja châo ...   อยากจะเช่า ...

how much does it cost per hour?
kâh châo chôo-mohng la
   tâo-rài?   ค่าเช่าชั่วโมงละเท่าไร

how much does it cost per day?
kâh châo wun la tâo-rài?   ค่าเช่าวันละเท่าไร

how much is the deposit?
kâh mút-jum tâo-rài?   ค่ามัดจำเท่าไร

**I'd like to go and watch some
  Thai boxing**
yàhk bpai doo moo-ay tai   อยากไปดูมวยไทย

SPORT

can we use the tennis court?
rao chái sa-năhm ten-nít
  dâi mái?   เราใช้สนามเทนนิสได้ไหม

is there a swimming pool
  around here?
tăir-o née mee sà wâi náhm mái?   แถวนี้มีสระว่ายน้ำไหม

letter	jòt-măi	จดหมาย
post office	bprai-sa-nee	ไปรษณีย์
recorded delivery	long ta-bee-un	ลงทะเบียน
send	sòng	ส่ง
stamp	sa-dtairm	แสตมป์
telegram	toh-ra-lâyk	โทรเลข

how much is a letter to England?
sòng jòt-măi bpai bpra-tâyt
ung-grìt tâo-rài?   ส่งจดหมายไปประเทศอังกฤษเท่าไร

I'd like four 9 baht stamps
kŏr sa-dtairm gâo bàht sèe
doo-ung   ขอแสตมป์ ๙ บาทสี่ดวง

I'd like six stamps for postcards
to England
kŏr sa-dtairm sòng bpóht-gáht
bpai ung-grìt hòk doo-ung   ขอแสตมป์ส่งโปสการ์ดไปอังกฤษหกดวง

is there any mail for me?
mee jòt-măi sŭm-rùp pŏm
(chún) mái?   มีจดหมายสำหรับผม (ฉัน) ไหม

I'm expecting a parcel from ...
pŏm (chún) koy hòr kŏrng jàhk ... ผม (ฉัน) คอยห่อของจาก ...

engaged	săi mâi wâhng	สายไม่ว่าง
extension	dtòr	ต่อ
number	ber toh-ra-sùp	เบอร์โทรศัพท์
phone (verb)	toh-ra-sùp	โทรศัพท์
phone box	dtôo toh-ra-sùp	ตู้โทรศัพท์
telephone (noun)	toh-ra-sùp	โทรศัพท์
telephone directory	sa-mÒOt măi-lâyk toh-ra-sùp	สมุดหมายเลขโทรศัพท์

is there a phone around here?
tăir-o née mee dtôo
 toh-ra-sùp mái?

แถวนี้มีตู้โทรศัพท์ไหม

can I use your phone?
kŏr chái toh-ra-sùp kŏrng
 kOOn dâi mái?

ขอใช้โทรศัพท์ของคุณได้ไหม

I'd like to make a phone call to Britain
yàhk ja toh-ra-sùp bpai tĕung
 bpra-tâyt ung-grìt

อยากจะโทรศัพท์ไปถึงประเทศอังกฤษ

I want to reverse the charges
kŏr hâi gèp ngern bplai tahng

ขอให้เก็บเงินปลายทาง

hello
hul-lŏh

ฮันโหล

could I speak to Khun Chanida, please?
kŏr pôot gùp kOOn chanida
 nòy dâi mái?

ขอพูดกับคุณชนิดาหน่อยได้ไหม

hello, this is Simon speaking
hul-lŏh pŏm 'Simon' pôot krúp

ฮันโหล ผมไซมอนพูดครับ

64

TELEPHONING

can I leave a message?
kǒr-fàhk sùng a-rai nòy dâi mái?　ขอฝากสิ่งอะไรหน่อยได้ไหม

do you speak English?
kOOn pôot pah-sǎh ung-grìt
　bpen mái?　คุณพูดภาษาอังกฤษเป็นไหม

could you say that again very
　very slowly?
pôot cháh cháh èek tee dâi mái?　พูดช้าๆอีกทีได้ไหม

could you tell him Jim called?
chôo-ay bòrk káo wâh 'Jim'
　toh mah　ช่วยบอกเขาว่าจิมโทรมา

could you ask her to ring
　me back?
chôo-ay hâi káo toh mah mài　ช่วยให้เขาโทรมาใหม่

I'll call back later
děe-o ja toh mah mài　เดี๋ยวจะโทรมาใหม่

my number is ...
ber toh-ra-sùp pǒm (chún) ...　เบอร์โทรศัพท์ผม (ฉัน) ...

he's not in
káo mâi yòo　เขาไม่อยู่

sorry, I've got the wrong
　number
kǒr-tôht pǒm (chún) toh ber pìt　ขอโทษ ผม (ฉัน) โทรเบอร์ผิด

it's a terrible line
sǎi née yâir mâhk　สายนี้แย่มาก

REPLIES

รอเดี๋ยวนะครับ (ค่ะ)　ror děe-o ná krúp (kâ)
hang on

ใครพูดครับ (คะ)　krai pôot krúp (ká)?
who's calling?

65

TELEPHONING

บาท	bàht	baht *(unit of currency)*
ตู้โทรศัพท์สาธารณะ	dtôo toh-ra-sùp săh-tah-ra-ná	public telephone box
ต่อ	dtòr	extension
รหัส	ra-hùt	code
เหรียญ	rĕe-un	coin
เสีย	sĕe-a	out of order
โทร.	toh	tel.
โทรศัพท์	toh-ra-sùp	telephone
โทรศัพท์ทางไกล	toh-ra-sùp tahng glai	long distance telephone

0	sŏon	๐	ศูนย์
1	nèung	๑	หนึ่ง
2	sŏrng	๒	สอง
3	săhm	๓	สาม
4	sèe	๔	สี่
5	hâh	๕	ห้า
6	hòk	๖	หก
7	jèt	๗	เจ็ด
8	bpàirt	๘	แปด
9	gâo	๙	เก้า
10	sìp	๑๐	สิบ
11	sìp-èt	๑๑	สิบเอ็ด
12	sìp- sŏrng	๑๒	สิบสอง
13	sìp-săhm	๑๓	สิบสาม
14	sìp-sèe	๑๔	สิบสี่
15	sìp-hâh	๑๕	สิบห้า
16	sìp-hòk	๑๖	สิบหก
17	sìp-jèt	๑๗	สิบเจ็ด
18	sìp-bpàirt	๑๘	สิบแปด
19	sìp-gâo	๑๙	สิบเก้า
20	yêe-sìp	๒๐	ยี่สิบ
21	yêe-sìp-èt	๒๑	ยี่สิบเอ็ด
22	yêe-sìp-sŏrng	๒๒	ยี่สิบสอง
30	săhm-sìp	๓๐	สามสิบ

31	săhm-sìp-èt	๓๑	สามสิบเอ็ด
32	săhm-sìp-sôrng	๓๒	สามสิบสอง
40	sèe-sìp	๔๐	สี่สิบ
50	hâh-sìp	๕๐	ห้าสิบ
60	hòk-sìp	๖๐	หกสิบ
70	jèt-sìp	๗๐	เจ็ดสิบ
80	bpàirt-sìp	๘๐	แปดสิบ
90	gâo-sìp	๙๐	เก้าสิบ
91	gâo-sìp-èt	๙๑	เก้าสิบเอ็ด
100	nèung róy	๑๐๐	หนึ่งร้อย
101	nèung róy nèung	๑๐๑	หนึ่งร้อยหนึ่ง
102	nèung róy sŏrng	๑๐๒	หนึ่งร้อยสอง
200	sŏrng róy	๒๐๐	สองร้อย
201	sŏrng róy nèung	๒๐๑	สองร้อยหนึ่ง
202	sŏrng róy sŏrng	๒๐๒	สองร้อยสอง
1,000	nèung pun	๑๐๐๐	หนึ่งพัน
2,000	sŏrng pun	๒๐๐๐	สองพัน
10,000	nèung mèun	๑๐๐๐๐	หนึ่งหมื่น
20,000	sŏrng mèun	๒๐๐๐๐	สองหมื่น
100,000	nèung săirn	๑๐๐๐๐๐	หนึ่งแสน
200,000	sŏrng săirn	๒๐๐๐๐๐	สองแสน
1,000,000	nèung láhn	๑๐๐๐๐๐๐	หนึ่งล้าน
100,000,000	nèung róy láhn	๑๐๐๐๐๐๐๐๐	หนึ่งร้อยล้าน

NUMBERS, THE DATE, THE TIME

1st	têe nèung	ที่หนึ่ง
2nd	têe sŏrng	ที่สอง
3rd	têe săhm	ที่สาม
4th	têe sèe	ที่สี่
5th	têe hâh	ที่ห้า
6th	têe hòk	ที่หก
7th	têe jèt	ที่เจ็ด
8th	têe bpàirt	ที่แปด
9th	têe gâo	ที่เก้า
10th	têe sìp	ที่สิบ

see also grammar section

what's the date (today)?
(wun née) wun têe tâo-rài? (วันนี้)วันที่เท่าไร

it's the fifth of April
wun têe hâh may-săh วันที่ห้าเมษา

(AD) 1994
kor sŏr nèung pun gâo róy
  gâo-sìp sèe ค.ศ. หนึ่งพันเก้าร้อยเก้าสิบสี่

what time is it?
gèe mohng láir-o? กี่โมงแล้ว

midnight
têe-ung keun เที่ยงคืน

midday
têe-ung wun เที่ยงวัน

1 a.m.
dtee nèung ตีหนึ่ง

1 p.m.
bài mohng บ่ายโมง

NUMBERS, THE DATE, THE TIME

2 a.m. dtee sŏrng	ตีสอง
2 p.m. bài sŏrng mohng	บ่ายสองโมง
3 a.m. dtee săhm	ตีสาม
3 p.m. bài săhm mohng	บ่ายสามโมง
4 a.m. dtee sèe	ตีสี่
4 p.m. bài sèe mohng	บ่ายสี่โมง
5 a.m. dtee hâh	ตีห้า
5 p.m. hâh mohng yen	ห้าโมงเย็น
6 a.m. hòk mohng cháo	หกโมงเช้า
6 p.m. hòk mohng yen	หกโมงเย็น
7 a.m. jèt mohng cháo/mohng cháo	เจ็ดโมงเช้า/โมงเช้า
7 p.m. tÔOm nèung	ทุ่มหนึ่ง
8 a.m. sŏrng mohng cháo	สองโมงเช้า
8 p.m. sŏrng tÔOm	สองทุ่ม
9 a.m. săhm mohng cháo	สามโมงเช้า
9 p.m. săhm tÔOm	สามทุ่ม

70

NUMBERS, THE DATE, THE TIME

10 a.m.
sèe mohng cháo   สี่โมงเช้า

10 p.m.
sèe tÔOm   สี่ทุ่ม

11 a.m.
hâh mohng cháo   ห้าโมงเช้า

11 p.m.
hâh tÔOm   ห้าทุ่ม

2.10 p.m.
bài sŏrng mohng sìp nah-tee   บ่ายสองโมงสิบนาที

3.15 p.m.
bài sǎhm mohng sìp-hâh
   nah-tee   บ่ายสามโมงสิบห้านาที

4.30 p.m.
bài sèe mohng krêung   บ่ายสี่โมงครึ่ง

4.40 p.m.
èek yêe-sìp nah-tee hâh
   mohng yen   อีกยี่สิบนาทีห้าโมงเย็น

7.45 p.m.
èek sìp-hâh nah-tee sŏrng
   tÔOm   อีกสิบห้านาทีสองทุ่ม

20.00 hrs
yêe-sìp nah-li-gah   ยี่สิบนาฬิกา

21.30 hrs
yêe-sìp-èt nah-li-gah sǎhm sìp
   nah-tee   ยี่สิบเอ็ดนาฬิกาสามสิบนาที

a *(see grammar)*

about *(approx)*
bpra-mahn ประมาณ

above
kâhng bon ข้างบน

accident
OO-bùt-dti-hàyt อุบัติเหตุ

adaptor *(for voltage)*
krêu-ung bplairng
fai fáh เครื่องแปลงไฟฟ้า

(plug)
bplúk ปลั๊ก

address
têe-yòo ที่อยู่

adult
pôo-yài ผู้ใหญ่

aeroplane
krêu-ung bin เครื่องบิน

after
lŭng หลัง

afternoon
dtorn bài ตอนบ่าย

afterwards
tee lŭng ทีหลัง

again
èek อีก

**against: I'm
against it**
pŏm (chún)
hěn mâi
dôo-ay ผม(ฉัน)ไม่เห็นด้วย

age
ah-yÓO อายุ

agent
ay-yên เอเย่นต์

ago
gòrn ก่อน

three days ago
săhm wun
gòrn สามวันก่อน

agree: I agree
pŏm (chún)
hěn dôo-ay ผม(ฉัน)เห็นด้วย

Aids
rôhk áyd โรคเอดส์

72

air
ah-gàht / อากาศ

air-conditioning
krêu-ung air / เครื่องแอร์

airmail: by airmail
sòng tahng
ah-gàht / ส่งทางอากาศ

airport
sa-nǎhm bin / สนามบิน

alarm clock
nah-li-gah bplÒOk / นาฬิกาปลุก

alcohol
lâo / เหล้า

alive
mee chee-wít yòo / มีชีวิตอยู่

all
túng mòt / ทั้งหมด

allergic to
páir / แพ้

allowed
un-nÓO-yâht / อนุญาต

all right: that's all right
mâi bpen rai / ไม่เป็นไร

almost
gèu-up / เกือบ

alone
kon dee-o / คนเดียว

also
dôo-ay / ด้วย

altogether
túng mòt / ทั้งหมด

always
sa-měr / เสมอ

ambulance
rót pa-yah-bahn / รถพยาบาล

America
a-may-ri-gah / อเมริกา

amp: 13-amp
sìp sǎhm airm / ๑๓ แอมป์

and
láir / และ

angry
gròht / โกรธ

ankle
kôr táo / ข้อเท้า

another (different)
èun / อื่น

another beer
bee-a èek kòo-ut
nèung / เบียร์อีกขวดหนึ่ง

answer
kum dtòrp / คำตอบ

antibiotic
yah
bpùti-chee-wa-ná ยาปฏิชีวนะ

antihistamine
yah airn-dtêe
hít-dta-meen ยาเอนตีฮิสตะมีน

antiseptic
yah kâh chéu-a ยาฆ่าเชื้อ

apartment
a-páht-mén อพาร์ตเม้นท์

appendicitis
rôhk sâi dtìng โรคไส้ติ่ง

apple
air-bpêrn แอปเปิล

appointment
nút นัด

apricot
ay-pri-kort เอพริคอท

April
may-săh-yon เมษายน

arm
kăirn แขน

arrest
jùp จับ

arrive
mah tĕung มาถึง

art
sĭn-la-bpà ศิลป

artist
sĭn-la-bpin ศิลปิน

ashtray
têe kèe-a
bOO-rèe ที่เขี่ยบุหรี่

ask
tăhm ถาม

asleep
norn lùp yòo นอนหลับอยู่

aspirin
airt-pai-rin แอสไพริน

asthma
rôhk hèut โรคหืด

at
têe ที่

at the station
têe sa-tăh-nee
rót fai ที่สถานีรถไฟ

at Lek's
têe bâhn kOOn
lék ที่บ้านคุณเล็ก

attractive
sŏo-ay สวย

August
sĭng-hăh-kom สิงหาคม

74

aunt (*elder sister of mother/father*)
bpâh ป้า

(*younger sister of father*)
ah อา

(*younger sister of mother*)
náh น้า

Australia
órt-sa-tray-lee-a ออสเตรเลีย

automatic
ùt-dta-noh-mút อัตโนมัติ

autumn
réu-doo bai-mái
rôo-ung ฤดูใบไม้ร่วง

awake
dtèun ตื่น

awful
yâir mâhk แย่มาก

axle
plao เพลา

B

baby
dèk òrn เด็กอ่อน

back
kâhng lǔng ข้างหลัง
(*of body*)
lǔng หลัง

come back
glùp mah กลับมา

go back
glùp bpai กลับไป

bad
mâi dee ไม่ดี

bag
gra-bpǎo กระเป๋า
(*suitcase*)
gra-bpǎo
dern tahng กระเป๋าเดินทาง

baggage check (*US*)
têe fàhk
gra-bpǎo ที่ฝากกระเป๋า

baker
kon tum
ka-nǒm-
bpung คนทำขนมปัง

bald
hǒo-a láhn หัวล้าน

ball
lôok born ลูกบอล

bamboo
mái pài ไม้ไผ่

75

bamboo shoot(s)
nòr mái   หน่อไม้

banana
glôo-ay   กล้วย

bandage
pâh pun plǎir   ผ้าพันแผล

Bangkok
grOOng-tâyp   กรุงเทพฯ

bank
ta-nah-kahn   ธนาคาร

bar
bah   บาร์

barber
châhng dtùt pǒm   ช่างตัดผม

bath
àhng àhp náhm   อ่างอาบน้ำ

bathroom
hôrng náhm   ห้องน้ำ

batter
bair-dta-rêe   แบตเตอรี่

be
bpen; (see grammar)   เป็น

beach
chai hàht   ชายหาด

beans
tòo-a   ถั่ว

beard
krao   เครา

beautiful
sǒo-ay   สวย

because
prór   เพราะ

bed
dtee-ung   เตียง

bedroom
hôrng norn   ห้องนอน

bee
pêung   ผึ้ง

beef
néu-a woo-a   เนื้อวัว

beer
bee-a   เบียร์

before
gòrn   ก่อน

begin
rêrm   เริ่ม

behind
kâhng lǔng   ข้างหลัง

Belgium
bpra-tâyt
bayl-yee-um   ประเทศเบลเยียม

bell
ra-kung ระฆัง
(for door)
grìng กริ่ง

below
dtâi ใต้

belt
kěm kùt เข็มขัด

bend
tahng kóhng ทางโค้ง

best: the best
dee têe sÒOt ดีที่สุด

better
dee gwàh ดีกว่า

between
ra-wàhng ระหว่าง

bicycle
jùk-gra-yahn จักรยาน

big
yài ใหญ่

bill
bin บิล

bird
nók นก

biro *(R)*
bpàhk-gah lôok
lêun ปากกาลูกลื่น

birthday
wun gèrt วันเกิด

biscuit
kÓOk-gêe คุกกี้

bit: a little bit
nít-nòy นิดหน่อย

bite *(insect etc)*
gùt กัด

black
sěe dum สีดำ

blanket
pâh hòm ผ้าห่ม

blind
dtah bòrt ตาบอด

blocked
dtun ตัน

blond
pǒm sěe
torng ผมสีทอง

blood
lêu-ut เลือด

blouse
sêu-a
pôo-yǐng เสื้อผู้หญิง

blue
sěe núm
ngern สีน้ำเงิน

boat
reu-a เรือ

body
râhng-gai ร่างกาย

boiled egg
kài dtôm ไข่ต้ม

boiled rice
kâo sǒo-ay ข้าวสวย

bomb
lôok ra-bèrt ลูกระเบิด

bone
gra-dòok กระดูก
(in fish)
gâhng bplah ก้างปลา

book
núng-sěu หนังสือ

bookshop
ráhn kǎi núng-sěu ร้านขายหนังสือ

boot (shoe)
rorng-táo รองเท้า
(car)
gra-bprohng tái rót กระโปรงท้ายรถ

border
chai-dairn ชายแดน

boring
nâh bèu-a น่าเบื่อ

boss
jâo nai เจ้านาย

both: both of
them
túng sǒrng ทั้งสอง

bottle
kòo-ut ขวด

bottle-opener
têe bpèrt
kòo-ut ที่เปิดขวด

bowl
chahm ชาม

box
hèep หีบ

boy
pôo-chai ผู้ชาย

boyfriend
fairn แฟน

bra
sêu-a yók
song เสื้อยกทรง

bracelet
gum-lai meu กำไลมือ

brake
bràyk เบรค

brandy
lâo brùn-dee เหล้าบรั่นดี

78

brave
glâh hăhn   กล้าหาญ

bread
ka-nŏm-bpung   ขนมปัง

break
dtàirk   แตก

breakfast
ah-hăhn cháo   อาหารเช้า

bridge (over river
etc)
sa-pahn   สะพาน

briefcase
gra-bpăo   กระเป๋า

bring
ao ... mah   เอา ... มา

Britain
bpra-tâyt ung-grìt ประเทศอังกฤษ

broken
dtàirk láir-o   แตกแล้ว

brooch
kĕm glùt sêu-a   เข็มกลัดเสื้อ

brother (older)
pêe chai   พี่ชาย
(younger)
nórng chai   น้องชาย

brown
sĕe núm dtahn   สีน้ำตาล

brush
mái gwàht   ไม้กวาด

bucket
tŭng   ถัง

Buddha
prá-pÓOt-
ta-jâo   พระพุทธเจ้า

Buddhism
sàh-sa-năh
pÓOt   ศาสนาพุทธ

Buddhist: he's
a Buddhist
káo núp tĕu
sàh-sa-năh   เขานับถือ
pÓOt   ศาสนาพุทธ

building
ah-kahn   อาคาร

bulb (light)
lòrt fai fáh   หลอดไฟฟ้า

bungalow
bung-gah-loh   บังกาโล

Burma
bpra-tâyt
pa-mâh   ประเทศพม่า

Burmese
pa-mâh   พม่า

79

burn (noun)
plǎir mâi · แผลไหม้

bus
rót may · รถเมล์

business
tÓO-rá · ธุระ

business trip
dern tahng bpai
tÓO-rá gìt · เดินทางไปธุรกิจ

bus station
sa-tǎh-nee rót may · สถานีรถเมล์

bus stop
bpâi rót may · ป้ายรถเมล์

but
dtàir · แต่

butcher
ráhn néu-a · ร้านเนื้อ

butter
ner-ee sòt · เนยสด

button
gra-dOOm · กระดุม

buy
séu · ซื้อ

by
doy-ee · โดย

by car
doy-ee rót yon · โดยรถยนต์

C

café
ráhn gǒo-ay
dtěe-o · ร้านก๋วยเตี๋ยว

cake
ka-nǒm káyk · ขนมเค้ก

calculator
krêu-ung kít
lâyk · เครื่องคิดเลข

calendar
bpà-dti-tin · ปฏิทิน

Cambodia
bpra-tâyt
gum-poo-
chah · ประเทศกัมพูชา

Cambodian
ka-mǎyn · เขมร

camera (still)
glôrng tài
rôop · กล้องถ่ายรูป
(movie)
glôrng tài
pâhp-pa-yon · กล้องถ่าย
ภาพยนตร์

80

can (noun)
gra-bpǒrng กระป๋อง

can: I/she can
chún/káo dâi ฉัน/เขาได้

I can't swim
pǒm (chún) wâi ผม(ฉัน)ว่าย
náhm mâi bpen น้ำไม่เป็น

Canada
bpra-tâyt
kairn-nah-dah ประเทศแคนาดา

canal
klorng คลอง

cancel
ngót งด

cap
mòo-uk หมวก

car
rót yon รถยนต์

card (business)
nahm bùt นามบัตร

careful: be careful!
ra-wung! ระวัง

car park
têe jòrt rót ที่จอดรถ

carpet
prom พรม

carrot
hǒo-a pùk-gàht
dairng หัวผักกาดแดง

cassette
móo-un tâyp ม้วนเทป
kah-set คาสเซ็ท

cassette player
krêu-ung lên
tâyp เครื่องเล่นเทป
kah-set คาสเซ็ท

cat
mair-o แมว

cauliflower
dòòrk ga-lùm-
bplee ดอกกะหล่ำปลี

cave
tûm ถ้ำ

ceiling
pay-dahn เพดาน

cemetery
bpàh cháh ป่าช้า

centigrade
sen-dti-gràyd เซนติเกรด

centre
sǒon glahng ศูนย์กลาง

certificate
bai rúp rorng ใบรับรอง

81

chain *(around neck)*
sôy kor — ส้รอยคอ

chair
gâo êe — เก้าอี้

change *(small)*
sàyt sa-dtahng — เศษสตางค์

change *(verb)*
bplèe-un — เปลี่ยน

change trains
bplèe-un rót fai — เปลี่ยนรถไฟ

cheap
tòok — ถูก

check *(US: money)*
chék — เช็ค

check *(verb)*
chék doo — เช็คดู

check-in
dtròo-ut chûng
núm-nùk — ตรวจชั่งน้ำหนัก

cheese
ner-ee kǎirng — เนยแข็ง

chemist
ráhn kǎi yah — ร้านขายยา

cheque
chék — เช็ค

cherry
cher-rêe — เชอร์รี่

chest
nâh òk — หน้าอก

chewing gum
màhk fa-rùng — หมากฝรั่ง

chicken
gài — ไก่

child
dèk — เด็ก

chilli
prík — พริก

chin
kahng — คาง

China
bpra-tâyt jeen — ประเทศจีน

Chinese
jeen — จีน

chips
mun fa-rùng
tôrt — มันฝรั่งทอด

chocolate
chork-goh-lairt — ช็อกโกเลต

chopsticks
dta-gèe-up — ตะเกียบ

Christmas
krít-sa-maht — คริสต์มาส

82

church
bòht โบส

cigar
si-gah ซิการ์

cigarette
bOO-rèe บุหรี่

cinema
rohng nǔng โรงหนัง

city
meu-ung เมือง

city centre
jai glahng meu-ung ใจกลางเมือง

clean *(adjective)*
sa-àht สะอาด

clean *(verb)*
tum kwahm sa-àht ทำความสะอาด

clever
cha-làht ฉลาด

clock
nah-li-gah นาฬิกา

close *(verb)*
bpìt ปิด

closed
bpìt ปิด

closet *(US)*
dtôo ตู้

clothes
sêu-a pâh เสื้อผ้า

clothes peg
mái nèep
pâh ไม้หนีบผ้า

cloud
mâyk kréum เมฆครึ้ม

clutch
klút คลัทช์

coat
sêu-a klOOm เสื้อคลุม

coathanger
mái kwǎirn
sêu-a ไม้แขวนเสื้อ

cockroach
ma-lairng
sàhp แมลงสาบ

coconut
ma-práo มะพร้าว

coconut milk
ga-tí กะทิ

coffee
gah-fair กาแฟ

cold
nǎo หนาว

83

cold: I've got a
cold
chún bpen wùt ฉันเป็นหวัด

collect call
toh-ra-sùp gèp โทรศัพท์เก็บเงิน
ngern bplai tahng ปลายทาง

colour
sĕe สี

colour film
feem sĕe ฟิล์มสี

comb
wĕe หวี

come
mah มา

come back
glùp mah กลับมา

come in!
chern kâo mah! เชิญเข้ามา

comfortable
sa-dòo-uk สะดวก

complicated
sùp-sŏn สับสน

computer
korm-pew-dter คอมพิวเตอร์

concert
gahn sa-dairng
don-dtree การแสดงดนตรี

condom
tŎOng yahng ถุงยาง

congratulations!
kŏr sa-dairng
kwahm yin
dee! ขอแสดงความยินดี

constipated
tórng pòok ท้องผูก

consulate
sa-tăhn gong-
sŎOn สถานกงสุล

contact lenses
korn-táirk
layn คอนแทคเลนซ์

cool
yen เย็น

corkscrew
têe bpèrt
kòo-ut ที่เปิดขวด

corner
hŏo-a mOOm หัวมุม

correct
tòok ถูก

cotton
fâi ฝ้าย

cotton wool
sŭm-lee สำลี

cough
ai ไอ

country
bpra-tâyt ประเทศ

course: of course
nâir-norn แน่นอน

crab
bpoo ปู

cream (to eat)
kreem ครีม

credit card
bùt kray-dìt บัตรเครดิต

crisps
mun fa-rùng tôrt มันฝรั่งทอด

crocodile
jor-ra-kây จรเข้

crowded
kon nâirn คนแน่น

cry
rórng hâi ร้องไห้

cup
tôo-ay ถ้วย

cupboard
dtôo ตู้

curry
gairng แกง

curtain
mâhn ม่าน

customs
sŎOn-la-gah-
gorn ศุลกากร

cyclist
kon tèep
jùk-ra-yahn คนถีบจักรยาน

D

dangerous
un-dta-rai อันตราย

dark
dum ดำ

date (time)
wun têe วันที่

daughter
lôok săo ลูกสาว

day
wun วัน

dead
dtai ตาย

deaf
hŏo nòo-uk หูหนวก

ENGLISH— THAI

death
gahn dtai   การตาย

decaffeinated
mâi mee kah-fay-in   ไม่มีคาเฟอีน

December
tun-wah-kom   ธันวาคม

deep
léuk   ลึก

delicious
a-ròy   อร่อย

dentist
mǒr fun   หมอฟัน

deodorant
yah dùp glìn dtoo-a   ยาดับกลิ่นตัว

depend: it depends
láir-o dtàir   แล้วแต่

dessert
kǒrng wǎhn   ของหวาน

diabetic
bpen rôhk bao
wǎhn   เป็นโรคเบาหวาน

dialect
pah-sǎh tìn   ภาษาถิ่น

dialling code
ra-hùt toh-ra-sùp   รหัสโทรศัพท์

diamond
pét   เพชร

diarrhoea
tórng sěe-a   ท้องเสีย

diary
sa-mÒÒt
bun-téuk   สมุดบันทึก
bpra-jum wun   ประจำวัน

dictionary
pót-ja-nah-
nÓÓ- grom   พจนานุกรม

die
dtai   ตาย

different
dtàhng   ต่าง

difficult
yâhk   ยาก

dining room
hôrng rúp-
bpra-tahn   ห้องรับประทาน
ah-hǎhn   อาหาร

dinner
ah-hǎhn yen   อาหารเย็น

direct
dtrong   ตรง

direction
tahng   ทาง

dirty
sòk-ga-bpròk   สกปรก

pí-gahn พิการ

disaster
hǎi-ya-ná หายนะ

disease
rôhk โรค

disgusting
nâh glèe-ut น่าเกลียด

disinfectant
yah kâh chéu-a
rôhk ยาฆ่าเชื้อโรค

distance
ra-yá tahng ระยะทาง

district (in town)
kàyt เขต

disturb
róp-goo-un รบกวน

divorced
yàh gun láir-o หย่ากันแล้ว

do
tum ทำ

that'll do nicely
dee láir-o ดีแล้ว

doctor
mǒr หมอ

dog
mǎh หมา

doll
dtÓOk-ga-dtah ตุ๊กตา

dollar
ngern dorn-lâh เงินดอลลาร์

door
bpra-dtoo ประตู

down: down there
kâhng lâhng
nôhn ข้างล่างโน่น

downstairs
kâhng lâhng ข้างล่าง

dream
kwahm fǔn ความฝัน

dress
sêu-a chÓOt เสื้อชุด

drink (noun)
krêu-ung
dèum เครื่องดื่ม

drink (verb)
dèum ดื่ม

drinking water
náhm dèum น้ำดื่ม

drive
kùp ขับ

driver
kon kùp คนขับ

87

driving licence
bai kùp kèe ใบขับขี่

drugstore *(US)*
ráhn kǎi yah ร้านขายยา

drunk
mao เมา

dry
hâirng แห้ง

dry-cleaner
ráhn súk hâirng ร้านซักแห้ง

duck
bpèt เป็ด

durian *(fruit)*
tÓO-ree-un ทุเรียน

E

ear
hǒo หู

early
ray-o เร็ว

earring(s)
dtÔOm hǒo ตุ้มหู

earth
lôhk โลก

east
dta-wun òrk ตะวันออก

easy
ngâi ง่าย

eat
gin kâo กินข้าว

egg
kài ไข่

egg noodles
ba-mèe บะหมี่

either ... or ...
... rěu ... ... หรือ ...

elastic
sǎi yahng yèut สายยางยืด

elbow
kôr sòrk ข้อศอก

electric
fai fáh ไฟฟ้า

electricity
fai fáh ไฟฟ้า

elephant
cháhng ช้าง

elevator
líf ลิฟท์

ENGLISH—THAI

else: something else
a-rai èek · อะไรอีก

embassy
sa-tăhn tôot · สถานทูต

emergency
chÒOk chěrn · ฉุกเฉิน

empty
wâhng · ว่าง

end (noun)
jòp · จบ

engaged (toilet)
mâi wâhng · ไม่ว่าง
(to be married)
mûn · หมั้น

engine
krêu-ung yon · เครื่องยนต์

England
bpra-tâyt ung-grìt · ประเทศอังกฤษ

English (language)
pah-săh ung-grìt · ภาษาอังกฤษ

English girl/woman
pôo-yĭng ung-grìt · ผู้หญิงอังกฤษ

Englishman
pôo-chai ung-grìt · ผู้ชายอังกฤษ

enough
por · พอ

that's enough
por láir-o · พอแล้ว

entrance
tahng kâo · ทางเข้า

envelope
sorng jòt-măi · ซองจดหมาย

epileptic
bpen rôhk lom
bâh mǒo · เป็นโรคลมบ้าหมู

Europe
yOO-rohp · ยุโรป

evening
dtorn glahng
keun · ตอนกลางคืน

every
tÓOk · ทุก

everyone
tÓOk kon · ทุกคน

everything
tÓOk yàhng · ทุกอย่าง

everywhere
tôo-a bpai · ทั่วไป

excellent (food, hotel)
yêe-um · เยี่ยม

89

exchange *(verb: money)*
lâirk
bplèe-un   แลกเปลี่ยน

exchange rate
ùt-dtrah lâirk
bplèe-un   อัตราแลกเปลี่ยน

exciting
nâh dtèun dtên   น่าตื่นเต้น

excuse me *(to get past)*
kŏr-tôht   ขอโทษ
(to get attention)
kOOn krúp (kâ)   คุณครับ (ค่ะ)
(pardon?)
a-rai ná?   อะไรนะ

exhibition
ní-tá-sa-gahn   นิทรรศการ

exit
tahng òrk   ทางออก

expensive
pairng   แพง

explain
ùt-ti-bai   อธิบาย

eye
dtah   ตา

eye shadow
kreem tah
nǔng dtah   ครีมทาหนังตา

F

face
nâh   หน้า

factory
rohng ngahn   โรงงาน

family
krôrp-kroo-a   ครอบครัว

famous
mee chêu
sěe-ung   มีชื่อเสียง

fan *(mechanical)*
pút lom   พัดลม
(hand-held)
pút   พัด

fantastic
yêe-um yôrt   เยี่ยมยอด

far *(away)*
glai   ไกล

farm
fahm   ฟาร์ม

fashionable
tun sa-mǎi   ทันสมัย

90

fast
ray-o เร็ว

fat (*person*)
ôo-un อ้วน

father
pôr พ่อ

faucet (*US*)
górk náhm ก๊อกน้ำ

faulty
pìt ผิด

favourite (*adjective*)
bpròht โปรด

February
gOOm-pah-pun กุมภาพันธ์

feel: I feel unwell
pŏm (chún) róo-
sèuk mâi sa-bai ผม(ฉัน)รู้สึก
ไม่สบาย

felt-tip pen
bpàhk-gah may-jik ปากกาเมจิก

fence
róo-a รั้ว

ferry
reu-a kâhm fâhk เรือข้ามฟาก

fever
kâi ไข้

few: few tourists
núk tôrng têe-o nóy นักท่องเที่ยวน้อย

a few
bâhng บ้าง

field
sa-năhm สนาม

filling (*tooth*)
ÒOt fun อุดฟัน

film (*for camera*)
feem ฟิล์ม
(*at cinema*)
năng หนัง

find
jer เจอ

finger
néw meu นิ้วมือ

finish (*verb*)
jòp จบ

fire
fai ไฟ
(*blaze*)
fai mâi ไฟไหม้

fire extinguisher
krêu-ung dùp
plerng เครื่องดับเพลิง

first
râirk แรก

first aid
gahn bpa-tŏm
pa-yah-bahn การปฐมพยาบาล

91

first class
chún nèung ชั้นหนึ่ง

first name
chêu ชื่อ

fish
bplah ปลา

fisherman
kon jùp bplah คนจับปลา

fishing
gahn jùp bplah การจับปลา

fishing boat
reu-a bpra-mong เรือประมง

fit (*healthy*)
fít ฟิท

fizzy
sâh ซ่า

flash
fláirt แฟลช

flat (*noun*)
fláirt แฟลต

flat (*adjective*)
bairn แบน

flavour
rót รส

flea
mùt หมัด

flight
têe-o bin เที่ยวบิน

floating market
dta-làht náhm ตลาดน้ำ

floor (*of room*)
péun พื้น
(*storey*)
chún ชั้น

flower
dòrk-mái ดอกไม้

flu
kâi wùt ไข้หวัด

fly (*insect*)
ma-lairng wun แมลงวัน

fly (*verb*)
bin บิน

folk music
don-dtree péun
meu-ung ดนตรีพื้นเมือง

follow
dtahm ตาม

food
ah-hǎhn อาหาร

food poisoning
ah-hǎhn bpen
pít อาหารเป็นพิษ

English	Phonetic	Thai
foot	táo	เท้า
on foot	dern bpai	เดินไป
football	fÓOt-born	ฟุตบอล
for	sŭm-rùp	สำหรับ
for you/me	sŭm-rùp kOOn/ pŏm (chún)	สำหรับคุณ/ผม(ฉัน)
I'm all for it	pŏm (chún) hĕn dôo-ay	ผม(ฉัน)เห็นด้วย
forbidden	hâhm	ห้าม
foreigner	chao dtàhng bpra-tâyt	ชาวต่างประเทศ
forest	bpàh	ป่า
forget	leum	ลืม
fork	sôrm	ส้อม
(in road)	tahng yâirk	ทางแยก

English	Phonetic	Thai
form (to fill in)	bàirp form	แบบฟอร์ม
fortnight	sŏrng ah-tít	สองอาทิตย์
forward (mail)	sòng dtòr	ส่งต่อ
fracture	gra-dòok hùk	กระดูกหัก
France	bpra-tâyt fa-rùng-sàyt	ประเทศฝรั่งเศส
free	ì-sa-rá	อิสระ
(of charge) free		ฟรี
French (language)	pah-săh fa-rùng-sàyt	ภาษาฝรั่งเศส
French fries	mun fa-rùng tôrt	มันฝรั่งทอด
Friday	wun sùk	วันศุกร์
fridge	dtôo yen	ตู้เย็น

ENGLISH—THAI

fried noodles *(Thai style)* pùt tai ผัดไทย
(Chinese style) pùt see éw ผัดซีอิ๊ว

fried rice
kâo pùt ข้าวผัด

friend
pêu-un เพื่อน

frog
gòp กบ

from: from Bangkok to Chiangmai
jàhk grOOng-tâyp จากกรุงเทพฯ
bpai chee-ung-mài ไปเชียงใหม่

front *(part)*
nâh หน้า

in front of
kâhng nâh ข้างหน้า

fruit
pǒn-la-mái ผลไม้

fry *(deep-fry)*
tôrt ทอด
(stir-fry)
pùt ผัด

full
dtem เต็ม

fun: have fun!
têe-o sa-nÒOk ná! เที่ยวสนุกนะ

funeral
ngahn sòp งานศพ

funny *(strange)*
bplàirk แปลก
(amusing)
dta-lòk ตลก

furniture
krêu-ung reu-un เครื่องเรือน

further
ler-ee bpai เลยไป

fuse
few ฟิวส์

G

garage *(repair)*
òo sôrm rót อู่ซ่อมรถ
(for parking)
rohng rót โรงรถ

garden
sǒo-un สวน

garlic
gra-tee-um กระเทียม

94

gas
gáirt แก๊ส
(gasoline)
núm mun น้ำมัน

gate
bpra-dtoo ประตู

gay
gra-ter-ee กระเทย

gear
gee-a เกียร์

gents *(toilet)*
bOO-ròOt บุรุษ

genuine
táir แท้

Germany
bpra-tâyt
yer-ra-mun ประเทศเยอรมัน

get *(obtain)*
dâi ได้

can you tell me
how to get to ...?
bòrk tahng bpai บอกทางไปที่ ...
têe ... nòy dâi mái? หน่อยได้ไหม

get back *(return)*
glùp กลับ

get off
long ลง

get up
dtèun ตื่น

gin
lâo yin เหล้ายิน

girl
pôo-yǐng ผู้หญิง

girlfriend
fairn แฟน

give
hâi ให้

give back
keun คืน

glad
yin dee ยินดี

glass
gâir-o แก้ว

glasses
wâirn dtah แว่นตา

gloves
tǒOng meu ถุงมือ

glue
gao กาว

go
bpai ไป

95

go away
bpai ไป

go away!
bpai hâi pón! ไปให้พ้น

go down
long bpai ลงไป

go in
kâo bpai เข้าไป

go out
òrk bpai ออกไป

go through
pàhn bpai ผ่านไป

go up
kêun bpai ขึ้นไป

God
pra-jâo พระเจ้า

gold
torng ทอง

Golden Triangle
săhm lèe-um
torng kum สามเหลี่ยมทองคำ

goldsmith
châhng torng ช่างทอง

good
dee ดี

good!
dee láir-o! ดีแล้ว

goodbye
lah gòrn ná ลาก่อนนะ

got: have you
got ...?
mee ... mái? มี ... ไหม

government
rút-ta-bahn รัฐบาล

grammar
wai-yah-gorn ไวยากรณ์

grandfather
(maternal)
dtah ตา
(paternal)
bpòo ปู่

grandmother
(maternal)
yai ยาย
(paternal)
yâh ย่า

grapefruit
sôm oh ส้มโอ

grapes
a-ngÒOn องุ่น

grass
yâh หญ้า

grateful
róo-sèuk
kòrp-kOOn   รู้สึกขอบคุณ

greasy
bpen mun   เป็นมัน

green
sěe kěe-o   สีเขียว

grey
sěe tao   สีเทา

ground floor
chún nèung   ชั้นหนึ่ง

group
glOOm   กลุ่ม

guarantee
bai rúp-rorng   ใบรับรอง

guest
kàirk   แขก

guide
múk-kOO-tâyt   มัคคุเทศก์

guidebook
kôo meu num
têe-o   คู่มือนำเที่ยว

guitar
gee-dtâh   กีต้าร์

gun (pistol)
bpeun pók   ปืนพก
(rifle)
bpeun yao   ปืนยาว

H

hair
pǒm   ผม

haircut
dtùt pǒm   ตัดผม

hairdresser
châhng dtùt
pǒm   ช่างตัดผม

half
krêung   ครึ่ง

half an hour
krêung chôo-a
mohng   ครึ่งชั่วโมง

ham
mǒo hairm   หมูแฮม

hamburger
hairm-ber-gêr   แฮมเบอร์เกอร์

hammer
kórn   ฆ้อน

hand
meu   มือ

handbag
gra-bpǎo těu   กระเป๋าถือ

handkerchief
pâh chét nâh   ผ้าเช็ดหน้า

hand luggage
gra-bpǎo těu   กระเป๋าถือ

handsome
rôop lòr   รูปหล่อ

happy
dee jai   ดีใจ

happy New Year!
sa-wùt dee bpee
mài!   สวัสดีปีใหม่

harbour
tâh reu-a   ท่าเรือ

hard (material)
kǎirng   แข็ง
(difficult)
yâhk   ยาก

hat
mòo-uk   หมวก

hate
glèe-ut   เกลียด

have
mee   มี

I have to ...
pǒm (chún)
dtôrng ...   ผม(ฉัน)ต้อง ...

hay fever
rôhk hèut   โรคหืด

he
káo;   เขา
(see grammar)

head
hǒo-a   หัว

headache
bpòo-ut hǒo-a ปวดหัว

headlights
fai nâh rót   ไฟหน้ารถ

hear
dâi yin   ได้ยิน

hearing aid
krêu-ung
chôo-ay fung   เครื่องช่วยฟัง

heart
hǒo-a jai   หัวใจ

heart attack
hǒo-a jai wai หัวใจวาย

heat
kwahm rórn   ความร้อน

heavy
nùk   หนัก

98

heel (*of shoe*)
sôn rorng táo   ส้นรองเท้า
(*of foot*)
sôn táo   ส้นเท้า

helicopter
hay-li-korp-dter   เฮลิคอปเตอร์

hello
sa-wùt dee   สวัสดี

help (*noun*)
kwahm chôo-ay
lĕu-a   ความช่วยเหลือ

help (*verb*)
chôo-ay   ช่วย

help!
chôo-ay dôo-ay!   ช่วยด้วย

her (*possessive*)
kŏrng káo   ของเขา
(*object*)
káo;   เขา
(*see grammar*)

herbs (*cooking*)
krêu-ung tâyt   เครื่องเทศ
(*medicine*)
sa-mŎOn prai   สมุนไพร

here
têe-nêe   ที่นี่

hers
kŏrng káo;   ของเขา
(*see grammar*)

hiccups
sa-èuk   สะอึก

high
sŏong   สูง

hill
kăo   เขา

hill tribe
chao kăo   ชาวเขา

him
káo   เขา

hip
sa-pôhk   สะโพก

hire: for hire
hâi châo   ให้เช่า

his
kŏrng káo   ของเขา

it's his
bpen kŏrng
káo;   เป็นของเขา
(*see grammar*)

hit (*verb*)
dtee   ตี

99

hitchhike
bòhk rót โบกรถ

hole
roo รู

holiday
wun yòOt วันหยุด
(public)
wun yòOt
râht-cha-gahn วันหยุดราชการ

Holland
bpra-tâyt hor-lairn ประเทศฮอลแลนด์

home: at home
têe bâhn ที่บ้าน
(in my country)
nai bpra-tâyt pŏm
(chún) ในประเทศผม(ฉัน)

go home
glùp bâhn กลับบ้าน

honey
núm pêung น้ำผึ้ง

hope (verb)
wǔng หวัง

horrible
nâh glèe-ut น่าเกลียด

horse
máh ม้า

hospital
rohng pa-
yah-bahn โรงพยาบาล

hospitality
gahn dtôrn
rúp kùp sôo การต้อนรับขับสู้

hostess (in bar)
pôo-yǐng bah ผู้หญิงบาร์

hot
rórn ร้อน
(to taste)
pèt เผ็ด

hotel
rohng rairm โรงแรม

hour
chôo-a mohng ชั่วโมง

house
bâhn บ้าน

how?
yung-ngai? อย่างไร

how are you?
bpen yung-ngai
bâhng? เป็นอย่างไรบ้าง

how many?
gèe? กี่

how much?
tâo-rài? เท่าไร

humid	
chéun	ชื้น

hungry: I'm hungry	
pŏm (chún) hěw	
kâo	ผม(ฉัน)หิวข้าว

hurry up!	
ray-o ray-o kâo!	เร็วๆ เข้า

hurt: it hurts	
jèp	เจ็บ

husband	
săh-mee	สามี

I

I (male)	
pŏm	ผม
(female)	
chún/	
dee-chún;	ฉัน/ดิฉัน
(see grammar)	

ice	
núm kăirng	น้ำแข็ง

ice cream	
ai dtĭm	ไอติ๋ม

idiot	
kon bâh	คนบ้า

if	
tâh	ถ้า

ignition	
fai krêu-ung	
yon	ไฟเครื่องยนต์

ill	
mâi sa-bai	ไม่สบาย

immediately	
tun-tee	ทันที

important	
sŭm-kun	สำคัญ

impossible	
bpen bpai mâi	
dâi	เป็นไปไม่ได้

in	
nai	ใน

in London	
nai lorn-dorn	ในลอนดอน

in English	
bpen pah-săh	
ung-grìt	เป็นภาษาอังกฤษ

is Somchai in?	
kOOn Sŏm-	
chai yòo mái?	คุณสมชายอยู่ไหม

included	
roo-um yòo	
dôo-ay	รวมอยู่ด้วย

ENGLISH—THAI

India
bpra-tâyt in-dee-a ประเทศอินเดีย

Indian
kàirk แขก

indigestion
ah-hăhn mâi yôy อาหารไม่ย่อย

industry
ÒOt-săh-ha-gum อุตสาหกรรม

infection
ah-gahn ùk-sàyp อาการอักเสบ

information
kào-săhn ข่าวสาร

injection
chèet yah ฉีดยา

injured
bàht jèp บาดเจ็บ

inner tube
yahng nai ยางใน

innocent
bor-ri-sÒOt บริสุทธิ์

insect
ma-lairng แมลง

insect repellent
yah gun ma-lairng ยากันแมลง

insurance
gahn bpra-gun pai การประกันภัย

intelligent
cha-làht ฉลาด

interesting
nâh sŏn jai น่าสนใจ

invitation
kum chern คำเชิญ

Ireland
ai-lairn ไอร์แลนด์

iron (metal)
lèk เหล็ก
(for clothes)
dtao rêet เตารีด

ironmonger's
ráhn kăi
krêu-ung ร้านขายเครื่อง
lèk เหล็ก

island
gòr เกาะ

it
mun มัน

it is ...
bpen ... เป็น ...

Italy
bpra-tâyt ì-dtah-lee ประเทศอิตาลี

102

J

jack *(car)*
mâir rairng
แม่แรง

jacket
sêu-a nôrk
เสื้อนอก

jam
yairm
แยม

January
mók-ga-rah-kom
มกราคม

jaw
kǎh-gun-grai
ขากรรไกร

jazz
jáirt
แจ๊ส

jeans
yeen
ยีนส์

jeweller's
ráhn kǎi krêu-ung
pét ploy
ร้านขายเครื่อง
เพชรพลอย

jewellery
pét ploy
เพชรพลอย

job
ngahn
งาน

joke
dta-lòk
ตลก

journey
gahn dern
tahng
การเดินทาง

have a good
journey!
têe-o sa-
nÒOk ná!
เที่ยวสนุกนะ

jug
yèu-uk
เหยือก

juice
náhm
pǒn-la-mái
น้ำผลไม้

July
ga-rúk-ga-
dah-kom
กรกฎาคม

junction *(road)*
tahng yâirk
ทางแยก

June
mí-tOO-nah-
yon
มิถุนายน

jungle
bpàh
ป่า

just *(only)*
tâo-nún
เท่านั้น

just two
sǒrng un
tâo-nún
สองอันเท่านั้น

103

K

key
gOOn-jair   กุญแจ

kidneys
dtai   ไต
(to eat)
krêu-ung nai   เครื่องใน

kill
kâh   ฆ่า

kilo
gi-loh   กิโล

kilometre
gi-loh-mét   กิโลเมตร

kind
jai dee   ใจดี

kiss *(noun, verb)*
jòop   จูบ

kitchen
hôrng kroo-a   ห้องครัว

knee
hǒo-a kào   หัวเข่า

knife
mêet   มีด

know
róo   รู้
(person)
róo-jùk   รู้จัก

I don't know
pǒm (chún)
mâi róo   ผม(ฉัน)ไม่รู้

L

ladder
bun-dai   บันได

ladies *(toilet)*
sa-dtree   สตรี

lady
pôo-yǐng   ผู้หญิง

lake
ta-lay sàhp   ทะเลสาบ

lamb *(meat)*
néu-a gàir   เนื้อแกะ

lamp
kohm fai fáh   โคมไฟฟ้า

language
pah-sǎh   ภาษา

Laos
bpra-tâyt lao ประเทศลาว

large
yài ใหญ่

last
sÒOt tái สุดท้าย

last year
bpee tê láir-o ปีที่แล้ว

late
cháh ช้า

laugh
hŏo-a rór หัวเราะ

laundry (to wash)
súk pâh ซักผ้า
(place)
ráhn súk pâh ร้านซักผ้า

law
gòt-măi กฎหมาย

lawn
sa-năhm yâh สนามหญ้า

lawyer
ta-nai kwahm ทนายความ

laxative
yah tài ยาถ่าย

lazy
kêe gèe-ut ขี้เกียจ

leaflet
bai bplew ใบปลิว

leak
rôo-a รั่ว

learn
ree-un เรียน

leather
nŭng หนัง

leave (behind)
tíng wái ทิ้งไว้
(go away)
jàhk bpai จากไป
(forget)
leum ลืม

left
sái ซ้าย

on the left (of)
tahng sái ทางซ้าย

left-handed
ta-nùt meu
sái ถนัดมือซ้าย

left luggage
tê fàhk
gra-bpăo ที่ฝากกระเป๋า

leg
kăh ขา

lemon
ma-nao มะนาว

lemonade
núm ma-nao น้ำมะนาว

lemon tea
núm chah sài
ma-nao น้ำชาใส่มะนาว

lens (camera)
layn เลนซ์

less
nói gwàh น้อยกว่า

lesson
bòt ree-un บทเรียน

letter (in mail)
jòt-mǎi จดหมาย

letterbox
dtôo jòt-mǎi ตู้จดหมาย

library
hǒr sa-mÒOt หอสมุด

licence
bai ùn-nOO-yâht ใบอนุญาต

lid
fǎh ฝา

lie down
norn นอน

life
chee-wít ชีวิต

lift (elevator)
líf ลิฟท์

light
fai ไฟ

have you got a
light?
mee fai mái? มีไฟไหม

light (not heavy)
bao เบา

light bulb
lòrt fai fáh หลอดไฟฟ้า

lighter
fai cháirk ไฟแช็ก

like (verb)
chôrp ชอบ

I would like
pǒm (chún)
kǒr ผม(ฉัน)ขอ

like (as)
měu-un เหมือน

lip
rim fěe bpàhk ริมฝีปาก

lipstick
líp sa-dtík ลิปสติก

listen (to)
fung ฟัง

litre
lít ลิตร

little
lék เล็ก

a little bit (of)
nít-nòy นิดหน่อย

live (*verb: be alive*)
mee chee-wít yòo มีชีวิตอยู่
(*in town etc*)
yòo อยู่

liver
dtùp ตับ

living room
hôrng rúp kàirk ห้องรับแขก

lock (*noun*)
gOOn-jair กุญแจ

lock (*verb*)
sài gOOn-jair ใส่กุญแจ

long
yao ยาว

a long time
nahn นาน

long-tailed boat
reu-a hǎhng yao เรือหางยาว

look: look (at)
doo ดู

look (*seem*)
doo měu-un ดูเหมือน

look for
hǎh หา

look like
doo měu-un ดูเหมือน

look out!
ra-wung! ระวัง

lorry
rót bun-tÓOk รถบรรทุก

lose
hǎi หาย

lost property office
têe jâirng
kǒrng hǎi ที่แจ้งของหาย

lot: a lot (of)
mâhk มาก

loud
dung ดัง

love (*noun*)
kwahm rúk ความรัก

love (*verb*)
rúk รัก

lovely
sǒo-ay   สวย

low
dtùm   ต่ำ

luck
chôhk   โชค

good luck!
chôhk dee!   โชคดี

luggage
gra-bpǎo   กระเป๋า

lunch
ah-hǎhn
glahng wun   อาหารกลางวัน

lungs
bpòrt   ปอด

M

mad
bâh   บ้า

magazine
nít-ta-ya-sǎhn   นิตยสาร

mail
jòt-mǎi   จดหมาย

make
tum   ทำ

make-up
krêu-ung
sǔm-ahng   เครื่องสำอาง

man
pôo-chai   ผู้ชาย

manager
pôo-jùt-gahn   ผู้จัดการ

mango
ma-môo-ung   มะม่วง

many
mâhk   มาก

map
pǎirn-têe   แผนที่

March
mee-nah-kom   มีนาคม

market
dta-làht   ตลาด

married
dtàirng ngahn
láir-o   แต่งงานแล้ว

mascara
mair-sa-kah-
rah   แมสคารา

massage
nôo-ut นวด

match (light)
mái kèet ไม้ขีด
(sport)
gahn kàirng kŭn การแข่งขัน

material (cloth)
pâh ผ้า

matter: it doesn't
matter
mâi bpen rai ไม่เป็นไร

mattress
têe norn ที่นอน

May
préut-sa-pah-kom พฤษภาคม

maybe
bahng tee บางที

me (male)
pŏm ผม
(female)
dee-chún /chún ดิฉัน/ฉัน

me too
pŏm (chún) ผม(ฉัน)ก็
gôr mĕu-un gun; เหมือนกัน
(see grammar)

meal
ah-hăhn อาหาร

measles
rôhk hùt โรคหัด

meat
néu-a เนื้อ

medicine
yah ยา

meeting
bpra-chOOm ประชุม

melon
dtairng tai แตงไทย

mend
sôrm ซ่อม

men's room
bOO-ròOt บุรุษ

menu
may-noo เมนู

message
kào ข่าว

metal
loh-hà โลหะ

metre
máyt เมตร

middle
glahng กลาง

milk
nom นม

mine
kŏrng pŏm (chún)　ของผม(ฉัน)

mineral water
núm râir　น้ำแร่

minute
nah-tee　นาที

mirror
gra-jòk ngao　กระจกเงา

miss *(train etc)*
dtòk　ตก

I miss you
pŏm (chún) kít
tĕung kOOn　ผม(ฉัน)คิดถึงคุณ

Miss
nahng-săo　นางสาว
*(see Thailand and
Things Thai)*

mistake
kwahm pìt　ความผิด

modern
tun sa-măi　ทันสมัย

monastery
wút　วัด

Monday
wun jun　วันจันทร์

money
ngern　เงิน

monk
prá　พระ

monsoon
mor-ra-sŎOm　มรสุม

month
deu-un　เดือน

moon
prá-jun　พระจันทร์

more
èek　อีก

no more ...
mâi ... èek　ไม่ ... อีก

I've no more ...
pŏm (chún)
mâi mee ...
èek láir-o　ผม(ฉัน)ไม่
มี ... อีกแล้ว

no more rice,
thanks
mâi ao kâo
èek kòrp-
kOOn　ไม่เอาข้าวอีก
ขอบคุณ

morning
dtorn cháo　ตอนเช้า

110

mosquito
yOOng ยุง

mosquito net
mÓOng มุ้ง

most (of)
sòo-un mâhk ส่วนมาก

mother
mâir แม่

motorbike
rót mor-dter-sai รถมอร์เตอร์ไซค์

motorway
tahng dòo-un ทางด่วน

mountain
poo-kǎo ภูเขา

mouse
nǒo หนู

moustache
nòo-ut หนวด

mouth
bpàhk ปาก

movie
nǔng หนัง

movie theater (US)
rohng nǔng โรงหนัง

Mr
nai นาย
(see Thailand
and Things Thai)

Mrs
nahng นาง
(see Thailand
and Things Thai)

much
mâhk มาก

muscle
glâhm néu-a กล้ามเนื้อ

museum
pí-pít-ta-pun พิพิธภัณฑ์

mushrooms
hèt เห็ด

music
don-dtree ดนตรี

must: I/she must
pǒm (chún) /
káo dtôrng ผม(ฉัน)/เขาต้อง

my
kǒrng pǒm
(chún); ของผม(ฉัน)
(see grammar)

111

N

nail *(in wall)*
dta-bpoo ตะปู

nail clippers
têe dtùt lép ที่ตัดเล็บ

nail file
dta-bai lép ตะไบเล็บ

nail polish
yah tah lép ยาทาเล็บ

nail polish remover
núm yah láhng lép น้ำยาล้างเล็บ

naked
bpleu-ay เปลือย

name
chêu ชื่อ

what's your name?
kOOn chêu a-rai? คุณชื่ออะไร

my name is Jim
pŏm chêu Jim ผมชื่อจิม

napkin
pâh chét meu ผ้าเช็ดมือ

nappy
pâh ôrm ผ้าอ้อม

narrow
kâirp แคบ

nationality
sŭn-châht สัญชาติ

natural
tum-ma-châht ธรรมชาติ

near
glâi ใกล้

near here
glâi ใกล้

the nearest ...
... têe glâi têe
sÒOt ... ที่ใกล้ที่สุด

nearly
gèu-up เกือบ

necessary
jum-bpen จำเป็น

neck
kor คอ

necklace
sôy kor สร้อยคอ

need: I need ...
pŏm (chún)
dtôrng-gahn ... ผม(ฉัน)ต้องการ ...

needle
kĕm เข็ม

112

negative (*film*)
feem   ฟิล์ม

nervous
dtèun-dtên   ตื่นเต้น

never
mâi ker-ee;   ไม่เคย
(*see grammar*)

new
mài   ใหม่

news
kào   ข่าว

newspaper
núng-sěu pim   หนังสือพิมพ์

New Year
bpee mài   ปีใหม่

next
nâh   หน้า

next to
dtìt gùp   ติดกับ

nice (*person etc*)
dee   ดี
(*place*)
sǒo-ay   สวย
(*food*)
a-ròy   อร่อย

night
glahng keun   กลางคืน

nightdress
chÓOt norn   ชุดนอน

no
mâi   ไม่

no ...
mâi mee ...   ไม่มี ...

I've no ...
pǒm (chún)
mâi mee ...   ผม(ฉัน)ไม่มี ...

no rice thanks
mâi ao kâo krúp
       ไม่เอาข้าวครับ
(kâ);   (ค่ะ)
(*see grammar*)

nobody
mâi mee krai   ไม่มีใคร

noise
sěe-ung   เสียง

noisy
nòo-uk hǒo   หนวกหู

non-smoking
hâhm sòop
bOO-rèe   ห้ามสูบบุหรี่

noodles
gǒo-ay
dtěe-o   ก๋วยเตี๋ยว

noodle shop
ráhn gŏo-ay dtĕe-o ร้านก๋วยเตี๋ยว

normal
tum-ma-dah ธรรมดา

north
nĕu-a เหนือ

nose
ja-mòok จมูก

not
mâi; ไม่
(see grammar)

notebook
sa-mÒOt สมุด

nothing
mâi mee a-rai ไม่มีอะไร

November
préut-sa-ji-gah-yon พฤศจิกายน

now
dĕe-o née เดี๋ยวนี้

number (house,
phone)
măi-lâyk หมายเลข

nurse (female)
nahng pa-yah-
bahn นางพยาบาล

O

October
dtOO-lah-kom ตุลาคม

of
kŏrng ของ

office
sŭm-núk
ngahn สำนักงาน

often
bòy bòy บ่อยๆ

oil
núm mun น้ำมัน
(motor)
núm mun
krêu-ung น้ำมันเครื่อง

OK
oh-kay โอเค

I'm OK
sa-bai dee สบายดี

old (people)
gàir แก่
(things)
gào เก่า

how old are you?
kOOn ah-yOO
tâo-rài? คุณอายุเท่าไร

114

I'm 25 years old
pŏm (chún)
ah-yÓO yêe-sìp
hâh bpee ผม(ฉัน)อายุ ๒๕ ปี

omelette
kài jee-o ไข่เจียว

on (on top of)
bon บน

one
nèung หนึ่ง

onion
hŏo-a hŏrm หัวหอม

only
tâo-nún เท่านั้น

open (adjective,
verb)
bpèrt เปิด

operation
gahn pàh dtùt การผ่าตัด

opposite: opposite
the ...
dtrong kâhm ... ตรงข้าม ...

optician
jùk-sÒO pâirt จักษุแพทย์

or
rěu หรือ

orange (fruit)
sôm ส้ม
(colour)
sěe sôm สีส้ม

orchestra
wong don-
dtree วงดนตรี

other
èun อื่น

our(s)
kŏrng rao; ของเรา
(see grammar)

out: she's out
káo mâi yòo เขาไม่อยู่

outside
kâhng nôrk ข้างนอก

over (above)
kâhng bon ข้างบน
(finished)
sèt เสร็จ

over there
têe-nôhn ที่โน่น

oyster
hŏy nahng
rom หอยนางรม

115

P

package
hòr หอ

packet (of
cigarettes etc)
sorng ซอง

paddy field
nah นา

page
nâh หน้า

pagoda
jay-dee เจดีย์

pain
kwahm jèp
bpòo-ut ความเจ็บปวด

painful
jèp bpòo-ut เจ็บปวด

painkiller
yah ra-ngúp
bpòo-ut ยาระงับปวด

painting
pâhp kĕe-un ภาพเขียน

palace
wung วัง

panties
gahng gayng
naisa-dtree กางเกงในสตรี

pants (US: trousers)
gahng-gayng กางเกง

paper
gra-dàht กระดาษ

parcel
hòr หอ

pardon?
a-rai ná? อะไรนะ

parents
pôr mâir พ่อแม่

park (noun)
sŏo-un
săh-tah-ra-ná สวนสาธารณะ

park (verb)
jòrt จอด

parking lot (US)
têe jòrt rót ที่จอดรถ

part
sòo-un ส่วน

party (celebration)
ngahn lée-ung งานเลี้ยง
(group)
glÒOm kon กลุ่มคน

116

pass *(mountain)*
chôrng kǎo ช่องเขา

passport
núng-sěu dern
tahng หนังสือเดินทาง

path
tahng ทาง

pavement
bàht wít-těe บาทวิถี

pay
jài จ่าย

peach
lôok pêech ลูกพีช

peanuts
tòo-a ถั่ว

pear
lôok pair ลูกแพร์

peas
tòo-a ถั่ว

pedal *(bicycle)*
kun tèep คันถีบ

pedestrian crossing
tahng máh-lai ทางม้าลาย

pen
bpàhk-gah ปากกา

pencil
din-sǒr ดินสอ

penicillin
yah pen-ni-
seen-lin ยาเพนนิซีลลิน

penknife
mêet púp มีดพับ

people
kon คน

pepper *(spice)*
prík tai พริกไทย
(red/green)
prík yòo-uk พริกหยวก

per cent
bper-sen เปอร์เซ็นต์

perfect
yôrt yêe-um ยอดเยี่ยม

perfume
núm hǒrm น้ำหอม

period *(woman's)*
bpra-jum
deu-un ประจำเดือน

person
kon คน

petrol
núm mun น้ำมัน

petrol station
bpúm núm mun ปั๊มน้ำมัน

phone (*verb*)
toh-ra-sùp โทรศัพท์

phone box
dtôo toh-ra-sùp ตู้โทรศัพท์

phone number
ber toh-ra-sùp เบอร์โทรศัพท์

photograph (*noun*)
rôop tài รูปถ่าย

photograph (*verb*)
tài rôop ถ่ายรูป

phrase book
kôo meu sŏn-ta-nah คู่มือสนทนา

Phuket
poo-gèt ภูเก็ต

pickpocket
ka-moy-ee lóo-ung
gra-bpăo ขโมยล้วงกระเป๋า

piece
chín ชิ้น

pill
yah mét ยาเม็ด

pillow
mŏrn หมอน

pin
kěm mÒOt เข็มหมุด

pineapple
sùp-bpa-rót สับปะรด

pink
sĕe chom-poo สีชมพู

pipe
tôr ท่อ
(*to smoke*)
glôrng yah sên กล้องยาเส้น

pity: it's a pity
nâh sŏng-săhn น่าสงสาร

plane
krêu-ung bin เครื่องบิน

plant
dtôn mái ต้นไม้

plastic
bplah-sa-dtìk ปลาสติค

plastic bag
tŎOng bplah-
sa-dtìk ถุงปลาสติค

plate
jahn จาน

platform (*station*)
chahn chah-lah ชานชาลา

play (*theatre*)
la-korn ละคร

118

play (verb)
lên เล่น

pleasant
sa-nÒOk สนุก

please (asking
for something)
kǒr ขอ
(asking someone to
do something)
chôo-ay ช่วย

yes please
ao krúp (kâ) เอาครับ (ค่ะ)

pleased
dee jai ดีใจ

pliers
keem bpàhk kêep คีมปากคีบ

plug (electric)
bplúk ปลั๊ก
(in sink)
jÒOk ÒOt จุกอุด

plum
lôok plum ลูกพลัม

pocket
gra-bpǎo กระเป๋า

poison
yah pít ยาพิษ

police
dtum-ròo-ut ตำรวจ

policeman
dtum-ròo-ut ตำรวจ

police station
sa-tǎh-nee
dtum-ròo-ut สถานีตำรวจ

polite
sOO-pâhp สุภาพ

politics
gahn
meu-ung การเมือง

polluted
bpen pít เป็นพิษ

poor
jon จน

pop music
don-dtree
pórp ดนตรีพ๊อพ

pork
néu-a mǒo เนื้อหมู

possible
bpen bpai dâi เป็นไปได้

post (verb)
sòng jòt-mǎi ส่งจดหมาย

postcard
bpóht-gáht โปสการ์ด

poster
bpoh-sa-dter โปสเตอร์

119

post office
bprai-sa-nee ไปรษณีย์

potato
mun fa-rùng มันฝรั่ง

pound (money)
bporn ปอนด์

prawn
gÔÔng กุ้ง

pregnant
mee tórng มีท้อง

prescription
bai sùng yah ใบสั่งยา

present (gift)
kǒrng kwǔn ของขวัญ

pretty
sǒo-ay สวย

price
rah-kah ราคา

priest
prá พระ

prison
kÓÓk คุก

private
sòo-un dtoo-a ส่วนตัว

problem
bpun-hǎh ปัญหา

prohibited
hâhm ห้าม

pronounce
òrk sěe-ung ออกเสียง

prostitute
sǒh-pay-nee โสเภณี

pull
deung ดึง

pump
sòop สูบ

puncture
yahng dtàirk ยางแตก

purple
sěe môo-ung สีม่วง

purse
gra-bpǎo
sa-dtahng กระเป๋าสตางค์

push
plùk ผลัก

put
sài ใส่

pyjamas
sêu-a gahng-
gayng norn เสื้อกางเกงนอน

ENGLISH—THAI

Q

question
kum tăhm — คำถาม

queue
kew — คิว

quick
ray-o — เร็ว

quickly
ray-o — เร็ว

quiet
ngêe-up — เงียบ

quite *(fairly)*
por sŏm-koo-un — พอสมควร

R

rabbit
gra-dtài — กระต่าย

radio
wít-ta-yÓO — วิทยุ

railway
tahng rót fai — ทางรถไฟ

rain
fŏn — ฝน

it's raining
fŏn dtòk — ฝนตก

raincoat
sêu-a fŏn — เสื้อฝน

rape
kòm kĕun — ข่มขืน

rat
nŏo — หนู

raw
dìp — ดิบ

razor
mêet gohn — มีดโกน

razor blade
bai mêet
gohn — ใบมีดโกน

read
àhn — อ่าน

ready
prórm — พร้อม

rear lights
fai lŭng rót — ไฟหลังรถ

receipt
bai sèt rúp
ngern — ใบเสร็จรับเงิน

reception *(hotel)*
pa-nàirk
dtôrn rúp — แผนกต้อนรับ

121

record *(music)*
pàirn
sĕe-ung
แผ่นเสียง

record player
krêu-ung lên pàirn
sĕe-ung
เครื่องเล่นแผ่น
เสียง

red
sĕe dairng
สีแดง

red-headed
pŏm dairng
ผมแดง

religion
sàh-sa-năh
ศาสนา

remember: I
remember
pŏm (chún)
jum dâi
ผม(ฉัน)จำได้

rent *(verb)*
châo
เช่า

repair
sôrm
ซ่อม

repeat
pôot èek tee
พูดอีกที

reservation
jorng
จอง

rest *(remaining)*
têe lĕu-a
ที่เหลือ
(sleep)
púk pòrn
พักผ่อน

restaurant
ráhn ah-hăhn
ร้านอาหาร

restroom *(US)*
hôrng náhm
ห้องน้ำ

reverse (gear)
gee-a tŏy lŭng
เกียร์ถอยหลัง

reverse charge call
toh-ra-sùp
gèp ngern
bplai
tahng
โทรศัพท์เก็บ
เงินปลายทาง

rheumatism
rôhk bpòo-ut
nai kôr
โรคปวดในข้อ

rib
sêe krohng
ซี่โครง

rice
kâo
ข้าว

rice field
nah
นา

rich
roo-ay
รวย

122

right *(side)*
kwǎh · ขวา

(correct)
tòok · ถูก

on the right (of)
tahng kwǎh · ทางขวา

ring *(on finger)*
wǎirn · แหวน

river
mâir náhm · แม่น้ำ

road
ta-nǒn · ถนน

roll
ka-nǒm-bpung · ขนมปัง

roof
lǔng-kah · หลังคา

room
hôrng · ห้อง

rope
chêu-uk · เชือก

rose
dòrk gOO-làhp · ดอกกุหลาบ

route
tahng · ทาง

rubber
yahng · ยาง

(eraser)
yahng lóp · ยางลบ

rubber band
yahng rút · ยางรัด

rubbish *(refuse)*
ka-yà · ขยะ

rucksack
bpây lǔng · เป้หลัง

rude
mâi sOO-pâhp · ไม่สุภาพ

rug
prom · พรม

ruins
sâhk sa-lùk
hùk pung · ซากสลักหักพัง

rum
lâo rum · เหล้ารัม

run
wîng · วิ่ง

123

S

sad
sâo — เศร้า

safe
bplòrt-pai — ปลอดภัย

safety pin
kĕm glùt — เข็มกลัด

salad
sa-lùt — สลัด

salt
gleu-a — เกลือ

same
mĕu-un gun — เหมือนกัน

sampan
reu-a sŭm-bpûn — เรือสำปั้น

sandal(s)
rorng táo dtàir — รองเท้าแตะ

sandwich
sairn-wít — แซนด์วิช

sanitary towel
pâh un-nah-mai — ผ้าอนามัย

Saturday
wun săo — วันเสาร์

sauce
núm jîm — น้ำจิ้ม

sausage
sâi gròrk — ไส้กรอก

say
bòrk — บอก

scarf (neck)
pâh pun kor — ผ้าพันคอ

school
rohng ree-un — โรงเรียน

scissors
dta-grai — ตะไกร

screwdriver
kăi koo-ung — ไขควง

sea
ta-lay — ทะเล

seaside: at the
seaside
chai ta-lay — ชายทะเล

seat
têe nûng — ที่นั่ง

seat belt
kĕm kùt
ni-ra-pai — เข็มขัดนิรภัย

second (in time)
wí-nah-tee — วินาที

see
hĕn — เห็น

124

sell
kǎi ขาย

sellotape *(R)*
sa-górt táyp สก๊อตเทป

send
sòng ส่ง

separate
dtàhng hàhk ต่างหาก

September
gun-yah-yon กันยายน

serviette
pâh chét bpàhk ผ้าเช็ดปาก

several
lǎi หลาย

sew
yép เย็บ

sexy
sek-sêe เซ็กซี่

shade: in the shade
nai rôm ในร่ม

shampoo
chairm-poo แชมภู

share *(verb)*
bàirng แบ่ง

shaving brush
bprairng tah
kreem gohn แปรงทาครีม
nòo-ut โกนหนวด

shaving foam
kreem gohn
nòo-ut ครีมโกนหนวด

she
káo; เขา
(see grammar)

sheet
pâh bpoo
têe norn ผ้าปูที่นอน

ship
reu-a เรือ

shirt
sêu-a chért เสื้อเชิ้ต

shoe(s)
rorng táo รองเท้า

shoe laces
chêu-uk pòok
rorng táo เชือกผูกรองเท้า

shoe polish
yah kùt rorng
táo ยาขัดรองเท้า

shoe repairer
kon sôrm rorng táo คนซ่อมรองเท้า

shop
ráhn ร้าน

go shopping
bpai séu kŏrng ไปซื้อของ

short (person)
dtêe-a เตี้ย
(time)
sûn สั้น

shorts
gahng-gayng kăh
sûn กางเกงขาสั้น

shoulder
lâi ไหล่

shower (wash)
fùk boo-a ฝักบัว

shy
ai อาย

sick: I feel sick
pŏm (chún)
róo-sèuk ja ผม(ฉัน)รู้สึกจะ
ah-jee-un อาเจียน

sidewalk
bàht wít-tĕe บาทวิถี

signature
lai sen ลายเซ็น

silk
măi ไหม

silver
ngern เงิน

silver foil
gra-dàht
dta-gòo-a กระดาษตะกั่ว

similar
mĕu-un เหมือน

simple
ngâi ง่าย

since (time)
dtûng-dtàir ตั้งแต่

sing
rórng playng ร้องเพลง

single (unmarried)
bpen sòht เป็นโสด

sister (older)
pêe săo พี่สาว
(younger)
nórng săo น้องสาว

sit down
nûng นั่ง

size
ka-nàht ขนาด

skin
pĕw ผิว

skinny
pǒrm ผอม

skirt
gra-bprohng กระโปรง

sky
fáh ฟ้า

sleep
norn lùp นอนหลับ

sleeper (train)
rót norn รถนอน

sleeping bag
tǒOng norn ถุงนอน

sleeping pill
yah norn lùp ยานอนหลับ

sleepy: I'm sleepy
pǒm (chún)
ngôo-ung norn ผม(ฉัน)ง่วงนอน

slide (photo)
sa-lai สไลด์

slim
pree-o เพรียว

slippers
rorng táo dtàir รองเท้าแตะ

slow
cháh ช้า

slowly
cháh ช้า

small
lék เล็ก

smell (with the nose)
dâi glìn ได้กลิ่น
(have a bad smell)
měn เหม็น

smile (verb)
yím ยิ้ม

smoke (noun)
kwun ควัน

smoke (verb)
sòop bOO-rée สูบบุหรี่

snake
ngoo งู

snow
hí-má หิมะ

so (big, slow etc)
jung ler-ee จังเลย

soap
sa-bòo สะบู่

sock(s)
tǒOng táo ถุงเท้า

socket
bplúk fai ปลั๊กไฟ

soft
nîm นิ่ม

127

soft drink
náhm kòo-ut นํ้าขวด

sole (of shoe)
péun rorng táo พื้นรองเท้า

some (pronoun)
bâhng บ้าง

somebody
krai ใคร

something
a-rai อะไร

sometimes
bahng tee บางที

son
lôok chai ลูกชาย

song
playng เพลง

soon
děe-o เดี๋ยว

**sore: I've got a
sore throat**
pǒm (chún) jèp kor ผม(ฉัน)เจ็บคอ

sorry
kǒr-tôht ขอโทษ

I'm sorry
pǒm (chún) sěe-a
jai ผม(ฉัน)เสียใจ

so-so
rêu-ay rêu-ay เรื่อยๆ

soup
sóOp ซุป

sour
bprêe-o เปรี้ยว

south
dtâi ใต้

soy sauce
núm see éw นํ้าซีอิ๊ว

Spain
bpra-tâyt
sa-bpayn ประเทศสเปน

spanner
gOOn-jair
bpàhk dtai กุญแจปากตาย

spare part(s)
a-lài อะไหล่

spark plug
hǒo-a tee-un หัวเทียน

speak
pôot พูด

do you speak ...?
pôot pah-sǎh พูดภาษา ... เป็น
... bpen mái? ไหม

speed limit
ùt-dtrah kwahm
ray-o   อัตราความเร็ว

spider
mairng mOOm   แมงมุม

spoke
sêe lór rót   ซี่ล้อรถ

spoon
chórn   ช้อน

sport
gee-lah   กีฬา

spring (season)
reu-doo bai mái plì   ฤดูใบไม้ผลิ

squid
bplah-mèuk   ปลาหมึก

stairs
bun-dai   บันได

stamp
sa-dtairm   แสตมป์

star
dao   ดาว

station (railway)
sa-tǎh-nee rót fai   สถานีรถไฟ

stay (in hotel etc)
púk   พัก

steak
néu-a sa-dték   เนื้อเสต็ก

steal
ka-moy-ee   ขโมย

steep
chun   ชัน

steering wheel
poo-ung
mah-lai   พวงมาลัย

sticky rice
kâo něe-o   ข้าวเหนียว

still (adverb)
yung   ยัง

I'm still waiting
pǒm (chún)
yung ror yòo   ผม(ฉัน)ยังรออยู่

stocking(s)
tǑOng nôrng   ถุงน่อง

stomach
tórng   ท้อง

stomach ache
bpòo-ut tórng   ปวดท้อง

stone
hǐn   หิน

stop (bus)
bpâi rót may   ป้ายรถเมล์

stop (verb)
yÒOt   หยุด

ENGLISH—THAI

stop!
yÒÒt!   หยุด

store
ráhn   ร้าน

storm
pah-yÓÓ   พายุ

story
rêu-ung   เรื่อง

straight: straight ahead
dtrong nâh   ตรงหน้า

strange (odd)
bplàirk   แปลก

stream
lum-tahn   ลำธาร

street
ta-nǒn   ถนน

string
chêu-uk   เชือก

stroke (attack)
bpen lom   เป็นลม

strong
kǎirng rairng   แข็งแรง

student
núk-sèuk-sǎh   นักศึกษา

stupid
ngôh   โง่

suddenly
tun-tee   ทันที

sugar
núm dtahn   น้ำตาล

suit
chÓÓt   ชุด

suitcase
gra-bpǎo
dern tahng   กระเป๋าเดินทาง

summer
nâh rórn   หน้าร้อน

sun
prá-ah-tít   พระอาทิตย์

sunburn
tÒÒk dàirt   ถูกแดด

Sunday
wun ah-tít   วันอาทิตย์

sunglasses
wâirn gun
dàirt   แว่นกันแดด

sunstroke
rôhk páir dàirt   โรคแพ้แดด

suntan lotion
kreem tah àhp
dàirt   ครีมทาอาบแดด

supermarket
sÒÒ-bper-
mah-get   ซุเปอร์มาร์เก็ต

ENGLISH—THAI

surname
nahm sa-gOOn   นามสกุล

sweet (noun)
tórp-fêe   ท็อฟฟี่

sweet (to taste)
wăhn   หวาน

sweet and sour
bprêe-o wăhn   เปรี้ยวหวาน

swim
wâi náhm   ว่ายน้ำ

swimming costume
chÓOt àhp náhm   ชุดอาบน้ำ

swimming pool
sà wâi náhm   สระว่ายน้ำ

swimming trunks
gahng-gayng wâi
náhm   กางเกงว่ายน้ำ

switch (electric)
sa-wít   สวิช

T

table
dtó   โต๊ะ

table tennis
bping bporng   ปิงปอง

take (remove)
ao ... bpai   เอา ... ไป

talk
pôot   พูด

tall
sŏong   สูง

tampons
tairm-porn   แทมพอน

tap
górk náhm   ก๊อกน้ำ

tape (cassette)
táyp   เทป

taste
rót   รส

taxi
táirk-sêe   แท็กซี่

tea
núm chah   น้ำชา

teach
sŏrn   สอน

teacher
kroo   ครู

team
teem   ทีม

teapot
gah núm
chah   กาน้ำชา

131

telegram
toh-ra-lâyk โทรเลข

telephone
toh-ra-sùp โทรศัพท์

television
toh-ra-tút โทรทัศน์

temple
wút วัด

tennis
tay-nit เทนนิส

tent
dten เต็นท์

terrible
yâir แย่

terrific
yôrt yêe-um ยอดเยี่ยม

Thai (adjective)
tai ไทย
(language)
pah-săh tai ภาษาไทย

a Thai, the Thais
kon tai คนไทย

Thailand (formal)
bpra-tâyt tai ประเทศไทย
(informal)
meu-ung tai เมืองไทย

than: uglier than
nâh glèe-ut gwàh น่าเกลียดกว่า

thank
kòrp-kOOn ขอบคุณ

thank you
kòrp-kOOn ขอบคุณ

that (adjective)
nún นั้น

that one
un nún อันนั้น

the
(see grammar)

theatre
rohng la-korn โรงละคร

their(s)
kŏrng káo; ของเขา
(see grammar)

them
káo เขา

then
gôr ก็

there
têe nûn ที่นั่น

there is/are ...
mee ... มี ...

is/are there ...?
mee ... mái? มี ... ไหม

there isn't/aren't ...
mâi mee ... ไม่มี ...

English	Thai (romanized)	Thai
thermometer	bpròrt	ปรอท
thermos flask	gra-dtìk náhm	กระติกน้ำ
these	née	นี้
they	káo; (see grammar)	เขา
thick	nǎh	หนา
thief	ka-moy-ee	ขโมย
thigh	nôrng	น่อง
thin (person)	pǒrm	ผม
thing	kǒrng	ของ
think	kít	คิด
thirsty: I'm thirsty	pǒm (chún) hěw náhm	ผม(ฉัน)หิวน้ำ
this	née	นี้
this one	un née	อันนี้
those	pôo-uk nún	พวกนั้น
thread	sên dâi	เส้นด้าย
throat	kor hǒy	คอหอย
through	pàhn	ผ่าน
throw	kwâhng	ขว้าง
throw away	tíng	ทิ้ง
thunderstorm	pah-yóO fǒn	พายุฝน
Thursday	wun pá-réu-hùt	วันพฤหัส
ticket	dtǒo-a	ตั๋ว
tie (necktie)	nék-tai	เน็คไท
tight	kúp	คับ
tights	tǒOng yai boo-a	ถุงใยบัว

time
way-lah   เวลา

on time
dtrong way-lah   ตรงเวลา

what time is it?
gèe mohng láir-o?   กี่โมงแล้ว

timetable
dtah-rahng
way-lah   ตารางเวลา

tin-opener
têe bpèrt
gra-bpŏrng   ที่เปิดกระป๋อง

tip
ngern típ   เงินทิป

tired
nèu-ay   เหนื่อย

tissues
pâh chét meu   ผ้าเช็ดมือ

to: I'm going to
Bangkok/the station
pŏm (chún) bpai   ผม(ฉัน)ไป
grOOng-tâyp/   กรุงเทพฯ/
sa-tăh-nee rót fai   สถานีรถไฟ

toasted bananas
glôo-ay bpîng   กล้วยปิ้ง

tobacco
yah sòop   ยาสูบ

today
wun née   วันนี้

toe
néw táo   นิ้วเท้า

together
dôo-ay gun   ด้วยกัน

toilet
hôrng náhm   ห้องน้ำ

toilet paper
gra-dàht
chum-rá   กระดาษชำระ

tomato
ma-kěu-a tâyt   มะเขือเทศ

tomorrow
prOOng née   พรุ่งนี้

the day after
tomorrow
wun ma-reun
née   วันมะรืนนี้

tongue
lín   ลิ้น

tonight
keun née   คืนนี้

tonsillitis
dtòrm torn-sin
ùk-sàyp   ตอมทอนซิลอั

too *(also)*
dôo-ay ด้วย

too big
yài gern bpai ใหญ่เกินไป

not too much
mâi mâhk gern
bpai ไม่มากเกินไป

too much
mâhk gern bpai มากเกินไป

tooth
fun ฟัน

toothache
bpòo-ut fun ปวดฟัน

toothbrush
bprairng sěe fun แปรงสีฟัน

toothpaste
yah sěe fun ยาสีฟัน

torch
fai chǎi ไฟฉาย

tourist
núk tôrng têe-o นักท่องเที่ยว

towel
pâh chét dtoo-a ผ้าเช็ดตัว

town
meu-ung เมือง

track *(US: station)*
chahn
chah-lah ชานชาลา

traditional
bpen ka-
nòp-tum เป็นขนบธรรม
nee-um -เนียม

traffic
ja-rah-jorn จราจร

traffic jam
rót dtìt รถติด

traffic lights
fai sǔn-yahn
ja-rah-jorn ไฟสัญญาณจราจร

train
rót fai รถไฟ

trainers
rorng táo
gee-lah รองเท้ากีฬา

translate
bplair แปล

travel agent's
trah-wern
ay-yen ทราเวิลเอเยนต์

traveller's cheque
chék dern
tahng เช็คเดินทาง

135

tree
dtôn mái   ต้นไม้

tremendous
wí-sàyt   วิเศษ

trip
têe-o   เที่ยว

trousers
gahng-gayng   กางเกง

true
jing   จริง

trunk (US: car)
gra-bprohng tái rót   กระโปรงท้ายรถ

try
pa-yah-yahm   พยายาม

T-shirt
sêu-a yêut   เสื้อยืด

Tuesday
wun ung-kahn   วันอังคาร

tunnel
OO-mohng   อุโมงค์

tweezers
bpàhk kêep   ปากคีบ

tyre
yahng rót   ยางรถ

U

ugly
nâh glèe-ut   น่าเกลียด

umbrella
rôm   ร่ม

uncle (older brother
of mother/father)
lOOng   ลุง
(younger brother of
father)
ah   อา
(younger brother of
mother)
náh   น้า

under
dtâi   ใต้

underpants
gahng-gayng
nai   กางเกงใน

understand
kâo jai   เข้าใจ

United States
sa-hà-rút
a-may-ri-gah   สหรัฐอเมริกา

136

university
ma-hăh-wít-ta-yah-lai มหาวิทยาลัย

unpleasant
năh rung-gèe-ut น่ารังเกียจ

until
jon จน

up: up there
yòo bon nún อยู่บนนั้น

upstairs
kâhng bon ข้างบน

urgent
dòo-un ด่วน

us
rao เรา

use (verb)
chái ใช้

useful
mee bpra-yòht มีประโยชน์

usually
tum-ma-dah ธรรมดา

V

vaccination
chèet wúk-seen ฉีดวัคซีน

valid
chái dâi ใช้ได้

valley
hÒOp kăo หุบเขา

van
rót dtôo รถตู้

vanilla
wá-ní-lah วานิลา

vase
jair-gun แจกัน

VD
wee dee วีดี

vegetables
pùk ผัก

vegetarian
kon mâi gin néu-a คนไม่กินเนื้อ

very
mâhk มาก

very much
mâhk มาก

video
wee-dee-o วีดีโอ

village
mòo bâhn หมู่บ้าน

vinegar
núm sôm น้ำส้ม

visa
wee-sah .... วีซ่า

visit *(verb: place)*
têe-o .... เที่ยว
(people)
yêe-um .... เยี่ยม

voice
sěe-ung .... เสียง

W

waist
ay-o .... เอว

wait
ror .... รอ

waiter
kon sérp .... คนเสริฟ

waitress
kon sérp .... คนเสริฟ

wake up *(oneself)*
dtèun .... ตื่น

walk *(verb)*
dern .... เดิน

walkman *(R)*
walkman .... วอร์คเมน

wall *(inside)*
fǎh .... ฝา
(outside)
gum-pairng .... กำแพง

wallet
gra-bpǎo
sa-dtahng .... กระเป๋าสตางค์

want
ao .... เอา

I want ...
pǒm (chún) ao ผม(ฉัน)เอา ...

do you want ..?
ao ... mái? .... เอา ... ไหม

war
sǒng-krahm .... สงคราม

warm:
it's warm
ah-gàht rórn .... อากาศร้อน

wash *(verb)*
súk .... ซัก
(oneself)
láhng .... ล้าง

washbasin
àhng láhng
nâh .... อ่างล้างหน้า

washing
powder
pǒng súk fôrk ผงซักฟอก

138

wasp
dtairn — แตน

watch *(for time)*
nah-li-gah — นาฬิกา

watch *(verb)*
doo — ดู

water
náhm — น้ำ

way: this way *(like this)*
yàhng née — อย่างนี้

can you tell me the way to the ...?
chôo-ay bòrk tahng bpai ... hâi nòy dâi mái? — ช่วยบอกทางไป ... ให้หน่อยได้ไหม

we
rao; — เรา
(see grammar)

weak
òrn-air — ออนเเอ

weather
ah-gàht — อากาศ

wedding
pi-tee dtàirng ngahn — พิธีแต่งงาน

Wednesday
wun pÓÓt — วันพุธ

week
ah-tít — อาทิตย์

weekend
wun săo wun ah-tít — วันเสาร์วันอาทิตย์

weight
núm-nùk — น้ำหนัก

welcome: you're welcome
mâi bpen rai — ไม่เป็นไร

well: he's well/not well
káo sa-bai / mâi sa-bai — เขาสบาย/ไม่สบาย

well *(adverb)*
gèng — เก่ง

west
dta-wun dtòk — ตะวันตก

wet
bpèe-uk — เปียก

what?
a-rai? — อะไร

what's this?
nêe a-rai? — นี่อะไร

wheel
lór — ล้อ

139

when?
mêu-rai?   เมื่อไร

where?
têe-nǎi?   ที่ไหน

which?
nǎi?   ไหน

white
sěe kǎo   สีขาว

who?
krai?   ใคร

whose: whose is
this?
nêe kǒrng krai?   นี่ของใคร

why?
tum-mai?   ทำไม

wide
gwâhng   กว้าง

wife
pun-ra-yah   ภรรยา

win
cha-ná   ชนะ

wind
lom   ลม

window
nâh-dtàhng   หน้าต่าง

windscreen
gra-jòk nâh
rót yon   กระจกหน้ารถยนต์

wine
lâo wai   เหล้าไวน์

winter
nâh nǎo   หน้าหนาว

wire
sǎi fai fáh   สายไฟฟ้า

with
gùp   กับ

without
doy-ee mâi   โดยไม่

without ice
mâi sài núm
kǎirng   ไม่ใส่น้ำแข็ง

woman
pôo-yǐng   ผู้หญิง

wonderful
yôrt yêe-um   ยอดเยี่ยม

wood
mái   ไม้

wool
kǒn sùt   ขนสัตว์

word
kum   คำ

work *(noun)*	
ngahn	งาน

work *(verb)*	
tum ngahn	ทำงาน

it's not working	
mun sěe-a	มันเสีย

world	
lôhk	โลก

worse	
yâir long	แย่ลง

wrench	
gOOn-jair bpàhk dtai	กุญแจปากตาย

wrist	
kôr meu	ข้อมือ

write	
kěe-un	เขียน

wrong	
pìt	ผิด

Y

year	
bpee	ปี

yellow	
sěe lěu-ung	สีเหลือง

yes	
(see grammar)	

yesterday	
mêu-a wahn née	เมื่อวานนี้

the day before yesterday	
wun seun née	วันซืนนี้

yet: not yet	
yung	ยัง

yoghurt	
yoh-gut	โยกัต

you	
kOOn;	คุณ
(see grammar)	

young *(man)*	
nÒOm	หนุ่ม
(woman)	
sǎo	สาว
(child)	
dèk lék	เด็กเล็ก

young people	
nÒOm nÒOm sǎo sǎo	หนุ่มๆ สาวๆ

141

your(s)
kŏrng kOOn;   ของคุณ
(see grammar)

Z

zero
sŏon   ศูนย์

zip
sìp   ซิบ

zoo
sŏo-un sùt   สวนสัตว์

STRUCTURE

For the Westerner, Thai grammar is relatively straightforward: word order in a sentence usually follows the pattern: *subject + verb + object*, while nouns and verbs both have a single fixed form, so the learner does not have to worry about singular and plural forms of nouns or verb tenses. There are also no articles - the or a - in Thai.

So for example, the word:

rót

can mean either car, cars, a car, the car(s), while the sentence:

káo bpai

can mean he comes, he is coming, he came, he will come and so on.

While from a Western viewpoint such apparent vagueness might seem likely to cause all kinds of misunderstandings, in actual fact, the context usually makes the speaker's intentions perfectly clear and, when it is necessary to be more specific, various words can be added to the sentence for clarification.

Using *NUMBERS* with nouns is a little different in Thai: a special counting word or *CLASSIFIER* has to be used, such as the word 'kon' person when referring to people:

pôo-yǐng sǒrng kon *(girls two person)* two girls

Notice that the word order is *noun + number + classifier*. If, however, you are referring to only one item, then the word 'nèung' one occurs after the classifier:

pôo-yǐng kon nèung *(girls person one)* one girl

GRAMMAR

While the classifier 'kon' is always used for referring to people, different classifiers are used for other types of noun. Some of the most common classifiers are:

bai   (for fruit, bowls, tickets)
dtoo-a   (for animals)
hàirng   (for places)
hôrng   (for rooms)
kun   (for vehicles)
lôok   (for round-shaped objects like balls, fruit)
un   (general classifier, used for nouns that have no specific classifier of their own or when you can't remember the specific classifier)

All units of measurement are regarded as classifiers; so, too, are containers such as cups, bowls, packages and so on.

> kŏr gah-fair sŏrng tôo-ay   two coffees, please
> *(request coffee two cup)*

> kŏr ka-nŏm káyk sèe chín   I'd like four cakes
> *(request cake four piece)*

> kŏr dtŏo-a bpai chee-ung-mài sŏrng bai   two tickets to
>   Chiangmai please
> *(request ticket go Chiangmai two + classifier for ticket)*

Although the context is often enough for the tense of *VERBS* to be understood, when it is necessary to be more specific about the time when the action occurs, various words can be added before the verb or after it.

The word 'láir-o' expresses the *PAST TENSE* and indicates completion of an action:

> pŏm doo láir-o   I have seen it
> rao gin kâo láir-o   we have eaten
> káo jài láir-o   he has paid

145

GRAMMAR

To indicate the past tense when it means used to or once did use 'ker-ee':

    rao ker-ee mee   **we used to have one/it**

The word 'ja' is used to express the *FUTURE* :

    chún ja bpai prÔOng née   **I'll go tomorrow**

The *PRESENT CONTINUOUS* or *PAST CONTINUOUS* is expressed by 'gum-lung':

    káo gum-lung gin kâo   **he is/was eating**

The word 'mâi' is added in front of the main verb to form the *NEGATIVE*:

chún mâi chôrp	I don't like it
mâi a-ròy	(it's) not nice (to eat)
pŏm mâi bpai	I'm not going (*said by a male speaker*)
rao mâi hěw	we're not hungry
rao mâi ker-ee bpai	we have never been (there)

Thai uses more *PRONOUNS* than English. There are, for example, numerous words for saying you in Thai, the appropriate word depending on the relative status of the speakers and the degree of familiarity between them. For the beginner, the following pronouns are the most useful:

pŏm	I, me (*male speaker*)
chún/dee-chún	I, me (*female speaker*)
kOOn	you (*singular and plural*)
káo	he, she, they, him, her, them
rao	we, us

146

GRAMMAR

Often, however, Thais will omit the subject pronoun. Thus, instead of saying 'pŏm mâi mee' I don't have any, they might simply say 'mâi mee'.

The same pronouns above are used with the word 'kŏrng' meaning of to indicate *POSSESSION*:

bâhn kŏrng káo   his/her/their house
(house of he)
gra-bpăo kŏrng chún   my bag *(said by a female speaker)*
(bag of I)

Often the word 'kŏrng' is omitted and Thais will simply say, 'bâhn káo' and 'gra-bpăo chún'.

The forms used for *POSSESSIVE PRONOUNS* are the same as those used to express the adjective above:

kŏrng chún   it's mine *(said by a female speaker)*

Thai uses the same relative pronoun 'têe' to mean who, which, and where:

kon têe kăi ...   the person who sells ...
nâhm têe chún gin   the water I drank
bâhn têe káo yòo   the house where he is living

ADJECTIVES occur after the noun they refer to:

sêu-a sŏo-ay   a pretty blouse
ah-hăhn pairng   expensive food
hôrng tòok   a cheap room

GRAMMAR

Adjectives in Thai should also be regarded as verbs: 'tòok', for example, means not only cheap but also to be cheap. The Thai verb to be - 'bpen' - is not used with adjectives:

> ah-gàht rórn   it's hot/the weather's hot
> *(weather hot)*

> hôrng lék   the room is small
> *(room small)*

BUT: káo bpen kroo he is a teacher
> *(he is teacher)*

The *COMPARATIVE* and *SUPERLATIVE* forms of adjectives are formed by adding the words 'gwàh' and 'têe sÒOt' respectively after the adjective:

> a-ròy gwàh   nicer *(to eat)*
> dee gwàh   better
> tòok têe sÒOt   cheapest
> dee têe sÒOt   best

There is no distinction between adjectives and *ADVERBS* :

> rót fai cháh   a slow train
> káo pôot cháh   he speaks slowly

Simple sentences can be transformed into *QUESTIONS* by adding the question word 'mái?' at the end:

> a-ròy   (it's) nice *(to eat)*
> a-ròy mái?   (is it) nice?

In Thai, there is no single word for *YES* and *NO*; if you want to answer yes to the question 'a-ròy mái?' you repeat the word, 'a-ròy'; and if you want to say no, you use the negative word 'mâi' in front of the verb:

148

a-ròy mái?	(is it) nice? *(to eat)*
- a-ròy	- yes
- mâi a-ròy	- no

Another common way of asking questions is to make a statement and then ask for confirmation that the statement is correct by adding 'châi mái?' to the end of the statement. Such questions are answered either 'châi' yes or 'mâi châi' no:

bpai prÔOng née châi mái?	(you're) going tomorrow, aren't you?
- châi	- yes
- mâi châi	- no

More specific question words are:

who?	krai?
krai bòrk?	who told you/him/her/them?
(who tell)	
what?	a-rai?
séu a-rai?	what did you/he/she/they buy?
(buy what)	
when?	mêu-rai?
glùp mêu-rai?	when will you/he/she/they/we/I return?
(return when)	
what time?	gèe mohng?
bpai gèe mohng?	what time are you/they/we going?
(go what time)	what time is he/she going?
	what time am I going?
where?	têe nái?
yòo têe nái?	where is it/he/she?
(situated where)	where are they?
why?	tum-mai?
tum-mai mâi bpai?	why aren't I/you/they/we going?
(why not go)	why isn't he/she going?

149

GRAMMAR

how much?	tâo-rài?
nêe tâo-rài?	how much is this?
(this how much)	
how long?	nahn tâo-rài?
yòo nahn tâo-rai?	how long did he/she/they stay?
(stay a long time	
how much)	
how many?	gèe (+ *classifier*)
mee lôok gèe kon?	how many children do you/they have?
(have child how	
many person)	how many children does he/she have?

Note that in the above examples, depending on the context, the verb could be translated into either the present, past or future tense.

In Thai, *POLITE PARTICLES* are used at the end of a sentence or question. Thai men will frequently add the word 'krúp' to indicate politeness; female speakers likewise will end sentences with the polite particle 'kâ' but the tone of the particle changes to a high tone 'ká' for questions. These particles have no translatable equivalent in English, where politeness is often conveyed by intonation.

Note that 'krúp' and 'kâ', when spoken in reponse to a question, mean yes.

The word 'kOOn' is a polite title used when *ADDRESSING* Thais. It should be placed in front of the first name, regardless of whether it is a male or female that you are speaking to. Surnames are never used when addressing someone.

In the phrase sections and dictionary of this book, the words 'kâ', 'dee-chún' or 'chún' in brackets replace the preceding word when the phrase is spoken by a female speaker.

150

3,600   Hotel
1,600   Bungalow

02   679 4570

Laura's mobil.
ORIGINATION
   070972608

Mine   079027973

HARRAP'S

Thai

PHRASE BOOK

Compiled by
LEXUS
with
David Smyth
and
Somsong Smyth

EDINBURGH   PARIS

First published in Great Britain 1993
by CHAMBERS HARRAP PUBLISHERS LTD
43-45 Annandale Street, Edinburgh EH7 4AZ, UK

ISBN 0 245 60378 6

Printed in Great Britain by Clays Ltd, St Ives